SPIN AND WIN

First published in 2008 by

CURRACH PRESS

55A Spruce Avenue, Stillorgan Industrial Park, Blackrock, Co. Dublin

www.currach.ie

1 3 5 4 2

Cover by bluett

Origination by Currach Press

Printed in Ireland by ColourBooks, Baldoyle Industrial Estate, Dublin 13

ISBN: 978-1-85607-949-5

The author has asserted his moral rights.

SPIN AND WIN

HOW POLITICIANS GET ELECTED

ANTON SAVAGE

CURRACH
PRESS

For Terry and Tom, the people I aspire to be

Contents

1

The Swarm

Politics in Ireland is all about the swarm. Ireland is the oddest little hive that doesn't have clear lines of demographic or geographic separation between its people. A Dubliner can meet a stranger in a pub in Killarney and within minutes, establish that they share a third cousin once removed in Cavan. Nor do we have clear lines of class. The guy who's the CEO of Aer Lingus could be in a pub in Tullamore talking to guys who've been cutting turf all day. You could be a commodities trader for CitiBank and your father could have been a brickie. We also have an interconnectedness in our media and geographical communities, in that half the people in Dublin don't come from Dublin and go home at the weekend. The same is true of all our cities.

That means we don't behave, electorally, the way the US does. Whereas it's possible to say that New Hampshire is a 'blue' state, nobody in their right minds would say that even Leitrim is an entirely Fianna Fáil county. The politician standing for election, as a consequence, can't pick a single interface with the electorate, whereas a US candidate – even for the presidency – can plan their interaction with voters around TV advertisements and pressing the flesh at a limited number of pre-planned rallies. In Ireland, you get elected through *every* interaction. You're going for election in Roscommon. How you act in a pub in

Dublin can have a significant impact on that. Your local radio performances will get picked up by the national media. Your national performances will be heard by the sons, daughters, brothers and wives of your voters, even if they no longer live in the constituency. The quality of your mother's cakes, baked in 1952 for the Pioneer association meetings, will be factored into some of your electorate's thinking, as will your party's policy on peak oil. You're a little bee in a crowded hive, where every single interaction and the ripple that interaction creates will matter.

Political life in Ireland is not about oratory. It's about interaction. Plural. Constant.

Our political system is geared to measure those interactions. We're one of the few countries in the world where you get elected based not on whether or not a voter likes you but on how *much* that voter likes you when they compare you, on a ballot paper, with twelve other candidates.

It's all about the swarm. Like ants.

The individual ant is a boring little fella. He doesn't read, he has no major insights, he has no holiday pictures to share. He lives a life with the constant burden of having a brain the size of a speck of dandruff. Likewise, the bee is intellectually limited, a dull chap whose only redeeming features above and beyond the ant are his natty pyjamas.

All being equal, evolution should have rid us of their dense and leggy presences a long time ago. Except that evolution has not supported the single ant or bee. It has supported the swarm. And the swarm is an extremely smart entity. It makes complex decisions about what temperatures are most conducive to foraging, where to set up shop, how to raise children, how to organise national defence and how to annex territory.

Any swarm is exponentially smarter than the sum of its

members. If you organised an EGM of your local beehive, sent out an agenda, pinned tiny name-badges to the pyjamas of those in attendance, gave a detailed PowerPoint presentation of the future plans for the hive and then put your proposals to a vote, you would get some mild buzzing and some dancing but nothing resembling a decision. Yet those same delegates make superb strategic and tactical decisions every day of their lives without even knowing it.

A lot of scientific types have been studying why lots of little dummies make a genius and they've found some intriguing things relevant to humanity. Relevant to humanity as it is *now*. Because humanity is different now from what it was in earlier centuries. We're not smarter. We haven't got any new emotions or radically increased insight. But we live in a world crucially divergent from the one we evolved to fit.

Cast your mind back through the strands of your own DNA to the fertile crescent in Mesopotamia. It is several hundred millennia BC and you're *Homo Sapiens*. Pretty much the same as you are now but with cheaper clothes. And no nylon.

You live in a small community where you know everyone. You deal with very little information; big teeth and stripes will eat me and it tastes like crap if I eat it. Big horns and tail will stand on me but worth the risk because it tastes groovy. Little red berry made Dave's wife throw up and die – don't eat red berries. Steve's wife is hot but Steve killed Bob for talking to her, so best to leave her alone. When the herds move north it's likely to start getting chilly, so good idea to skin something for a coat.

Some anthropologists have a theory that the reason we have such massive brains is not because they made us better hunters or gatherers, but because they allowed us to deal with big social groups, such as have been around since long before nylon. People with small brains couldn't stay on top of all the interrelations in a big network of people. Bob had a little brain. He chatted up Steve's wife in front of Helen. Helen was married to Peter. Peter was Steve's brother. They gossiped. Bob couldn't keep all those interactions in his head, so it came as a total shock to him when Steve removed that head from his shoulders.

The only constant correlation between animal activity and relative brain-size seems to relate to the size of the social group the animal operates within. Little brain: small group of mates; big brain: everyone's pal.

The reason for this is that interrelationships are tricky and take an enormous amount of brainpower to stay on top of (look at Bob). Take your own family; you need to know if your husband likes your mother, your father, your brothers and sisters. You then need to know if your mother, father, brothers and sisters like your husband. You then need to know which of your brothers and sisters don't like each other and which of them is your mother's favourite and your father's favourite. You then need to understand that the reason one of your brothers doesn't like your husband is because he's friends with your sister who is your dad's favourite. Then you need to know how you feel about your husband's family and how they feel about you and him. And how he feels about your relationship with each of them. And then you need to start working out how each of his family feels about each member of your family and vice versa.

And we haven't even got to cousins, children, grandparents or second relationships, never mind friends and acquaintances.

Hence we developed big brains.

But by modern standards our brains are not designed for what we do. We're wired for a relatively tight social group, living in a limited geographical region, with fairly fixed external stimuli and with limited external information as a basis for thought and decision. We are wired for relatively quick gut decisions: *Stripy thing! Runnn!* Not for complex reasoning.

Yet now we live in a world where we are bombarded with more information every hour than we would get in a lifetime in the Fertile Crescent. One Sunday newspaper has more raw data in it than a medieval scholar would have come across in his entire life. Google will offer us ten million hits for Paris Hilton. One single day's satellite broadcasting (roughly 10,000 hours of programming) would take fifteen years to watch if you did nothing but watch TV for every waking hour.

We tell ourselves 'It's OK. I can process it all, filter out the noise, pick the important bits and make rational, reasonable decisions.'

Nonsense.

Our solution to all this has been to discard data. Travel section of the *Sunday Times*? I already have a place in Spain. Kevin Myers? Never read him. *Lifetime*? Television for idiots.

We don't sample, consider, reflect and then dispose. We dispose at source. Human beings never used to do this. Our ancestors couldn't afford to dispose of information at source because the risks were too high. The songs learned by aboriginal children in Australia were melodic maps. They sang of where watering holes were, of where animals migrated, of where shelter could be found. The child who disposed of the song – and of the information it carried – died in the desert.

Now we have so much information coming at us every day that if we actually tried to memorise or react to all it, we'd die in the deluge. We are forced to consciously ignore much of the information we receive and therefore unconsciously outsource much of our decision-making.

Malcolm Gladwell nudged at this in his book *The Tipping Point*, where he wrote of small factors creating massive consumer movements. But most readers took from that book insights about marketing rather than decision-making. The reality is that humans now make very good swarm decisions based on most of the individuals within the swarm having about as much data and expertise as a bee has about choice of hive.

Peter Miller, writing in *National Geographic* magazine, explains how researchers did tests to establish how bee swarms make decisions about moving hives.

In one test they put out five nest boxes, four that weren't quite big enough and one that was just about perfect. Scout bees soon appeared at all five. When they returned to the swarm, each performed a waggle dance urging other scouts to go have a look. (These dances include a code giving directions to a box's location.) The vigour of each dance reflected the scout's enthusiasm for the site.

After a while, dozens of scouts were dancing their little feet off, some for one site, some for another and a small cloud of bees was buzzing around each box. The decisive moment didn't take place in the main cluster of bees but out at the boxes, where scouts were building up. As soon as the number of scouts visible near the entrance to a box reached about fifteen – a threshold confirmed by other experiments – the bees at that box sensed that a quorum had been reached and they returned to the swarm with the news.

In many ways, that is how humans now operate. Look at new websites. Web development is one of those areas where lots of people have lots of expertise but few can guarantee that their new site design will be the next Facebook. Why? Because standard rules of marketing and product-selling don't apply. You have a global audience of individuals, all with their own personal tastes, needs and experiences. They will not be as cross-saleable as within standard forms of media. For example an advertiser will have a fair shot at knowing that if you're watching *Top Gear* you will be interested in new cars, so they'll advertise their new roadster on UKG2's repeat of the programme. But if you are selling YouTube, where do you advertise? To whom? If you are selling eBay, how do you get customers?

Google has responded to this new human reality in a fascinating way; they have created Google Labs, a chunk of their operation where tame nerds develop stuff and then put it on their site and see who bites. Google Earth was such a product. It stormed the world because it got swarmed, not because it got advertised. Google Sketch-Up and Google Notebook are also (arguably more useful) Google Lab products, yet world domination hasn't happened for them, maybe because the scout bees didn't dance hard enough or because the fifteen needed for a quorum were busy networking on Facebook.

Such decision-making seems to be a devaluation of the intellect unique to humans but in most instances the swarm makes very good decisions. (Google is a better search engine than most of its competitors, YouTube is a highly addictive and entertaining site, Google Earth is revealing and hugely useful.) In the same way people are wary of decisions made by a swarm, because they're not 'thought out', they can be over-confident about decisions that are, apparently, thought out.

For starters, because we so value our individual brainpower, we rush to judgement. Sometimes the wrong judgement.

Proving this point, a famous psychological experiment asks people to choose which of two flight insurance policies they would buy (at the same price) a) a policy that pays out a million if they are killed in a plane crash or b) a policy that pays out a million if they are killed in a plane crash as a result of a terrorist attack.

The majority of respondents pick the second option despite its being a minor sub-set of the entirety of the first option. If you have an insurance policy that promises to pay out a million if your plane crashes, it pays the money out no matter what causes the crash. If a hamster eats the pilot's brain, your million is on its way to your family. Ditto if there's a terrorist attack.

So by picking the second option, what you're actually saying is: 'I don't want my family to get a bean if it's mechanical failure that causes my plane to go down, or a mid-air collision or bad weather or a hamster attack on the pilot's brain.'

Poor decision.

Dr Drew Westen writes extensively about this kind of poor decision-making in his book *The Political Brain*. Dr Westen did a number of psychological experiments in which he was able to show how voters could reverse the meaning of even the most declarative statement to fit with their bias. Play a Democrat a tape of a Democratic candidate clearly contradicting themselves, and the voter will infer justification for the contradiction that simply doesn't exist. Westen's research is the scientific proof of the cliché that people hear what they want to hear.

Even if people have no preordained political bias, their capacity to reason is easily swayed by context. Several studies have shown that diners will make judgements about how things taste based on the context in which they eat; an oyster eaten on a harbour wall will 'taste' better than one eaten at your desk in work. Similarly, crisps 'taste' better if the person eating them has the sound of the crisp-crunch amplified and played back to them while they eat. It is this capacity for context to define judgement that allows legislation like the US 'Patriot Act' or the 'No Child Left Behind' education programme to pass. The former has been criticised for removing basic civil liberties like the right to trial or the requirement for probable cause before warrants are issued or investigations undertaken. The latter was criticised for making swingeing cuts in education funding. Most of the criticisms were ignored, largely because it's difficult to criticise something that is put in the context of patriotism or support of children. Few would admit that their objective analysis was influenced by context, but just like the oyster on the harbour wall, the patriot act 'tastes' better because of its name.

All in all, humans have a unique gift for rationalising bad decisions *post factum*. Take what happened when a US Navy vessel shot down a civilian Airbus over the Persian Gulf. The radar operator called the shot because his instrumentation told him that the aircraft had moved into an aggressive steep dive, which led him to believe it was hostile. When the incident was investigated, officials discovered that his belief that the aircraft was hostile had led the operator to misread his instruments, which were actually indicating a steady climb. There is a posh term for this: scenario fulfillment – the capacity to change reality to fit your preconceived notions.

Poor decision.

And this is where human swarms are so useful. They rarely make bad decisions. Even if those decisions are largely uninformed.

Take the run on Northern Rock.

Most of the people who deposited money in a given bank were unlikely to know a great deal about international financial markets. Northern Rock depositors were unlikely to know about the run on Finland's banks that brought about the collapse of the

Finnish banking sector. They were, at the time, unlikely to have known about Northern Rock's exposure to the US sub-prime mortgage market. In fact they were unlikely, back then, to know what a sub-prime market was. They were also unlikely to know the difference between a short-term liquidity/cashflow problem and an intrinsic failing in a business model with concurrent exposure to risk. They were unlikely to know on what grounds a bank of last resort will extend an emergency loan. In fact they were unlikely to know what a bank of last resort was.

Some knew all those things. Most did not.

So why then did they queue for hours in the cold outside the branches of the bank to get their money? What rational grounds could they possibly have had to make such a decision?

None.

Aha! It was the media. Yep. To an extent. But the fact that the media reported an over-exposure to the US sub-prime market did not cause uninformed savers to jump in the car. The media reporting that *some savers had already withdrawn their money* caused the run. The swarm reacts to the reports of a quorum. It reacts to fifteen bees standing on the entrance of banking-hives.

The significance of all this is that anybody planning a political career needs to seek to influence the behaviour of the swarm. They'll be inundated with advisers and helpers who will tell them it's all about canvassing. Or it's all about media. Or it's all about name-recognition. Or it's all about image. Or it's all about networking.

It's actually about all of them and none of them.

2

THE BLACK SWAN EFFECT

The first question an aspiring politician needs to ask themselves is: do I really want this job?

People go into politics for three common reasons. Some of them are DNA politicians. It runs in the family and they inherit it. Some of them do it because they actually have a desire to make a difference to stuff. And some of them do it because they got vaguely involved at a young level and liked both the whiff of cordite and the sense of popularity.

It's often suggested that the most successful politicians are those who *don't* have a dream, who *don't* want to change the world. Any reading of politics shows that the Law of Unintended Consequences is never fully appreciated by dream-carrying politicians. If you enter politics with a desire to change the world, your definition of what changing the world means tends to be a little wide in scope and you are likely to be disappointed.

If you have a better understanding of how the world works you'll know that change is a little thing that happens around the edges and if enough little things around the edges happen a big thing will happen. Aspiring politicians need to realise that they're joining a movement which was established (in most cases) long before they were born. They are becoming part of a story which began before they existed and is likely to continue long after they have departed. So the urge to reach a point where you can say, 'And they all lived happily ever after thanks to what I did,' is one best damped down.

Instead, new politicians should realise that they're climbing on to something going in a particular direction, like an ocean liner heading for New York, and that it will eventually get there. Its getting there will not be greatly assisted by your handful of bright ideas but if you start grabbing the wheel and tweaking, you could endanger orderly progress.

The reason young politicians arrive in Leinster House with a bagful of grandiose dreams is that most biographies, whether about politicians or business figures, tend to isolate the big hairy ideas their subject had and focus on how he or she drove them. Why are they full of that kind of mythology? Because that's what readers want. The people who buy management books, business books or self-help bestsellers are always seeking the silver-bullet answer that made this guy successful. Thousands of readers then follow the guy's Seven Steps or Ten Tips and get nowhere but this reality never dampens the publics's appetite for silver-bullet solutions.

The reality behind monumentally successful politicians or business executives is always the same. Success comes from a combination of factors: the politicians' or business people's own level of dedication; their own brainpower; their capacity to drag useful people along with them; the reality of what is happening in the company or country; and a truckload of luck.

Extraordinary success, the success that makes you a party leader or a multimillionaire or a top CEO, usually has much more to do with luck than the party leader, multimillionaire or top CEO would like to accept. Nassim Nicholas Taleb has written a number of fascinating books on this theme. Taleb is a professor of philosophy and a very successful Wall Street trader. He writes about how big a part luck, bad or good, plays in our lives and how we persist in ignoring this.

Taleb talks of the 'black swan effect'. The black swan is a metaphor for how one event can radically change a person's life or even the world. For millennia, swans were white. Until the mid-19th century, when Australia was populated and black swans were discovered. That first black swan destroyed everything humanity understood about swans. You couldn't rely on them to be white any longer.

In geopolitical terms, 9/11 was a black swan. It was an event so far outside the predictable norms that nobody was prepared for it, nobody was insured against it and it instantly and comprehensively changed our view of the world we live in. The buildings hit in 9/11 – the Twin Towers and the Pentagon – housed the world's premier military and civilian risk analysts. They housed the best predictors of markets and military movements. All these people failed to predict the event which had a bigger impact on the markets and the military than any other in the previous half-century. If they had, they wouldn't have been there when it happened.

This is Taleb's thesis: we worry all the time about the minor and predictable and miss the major but less predictable. We failed to anticipate the fall of communism (the planet lost a major power without anticipating the collapse of the world order as we'd known it), Black Monday, SARS, avian flu, the war in Afghanistan, the sub-prime collapse and the recent global credit crunch.

The point Taleb makes is that seemingly unpredictable events are in fact predictable. We ignore them when we make predictions because they are so big and important. Black swans happen constantly: think of Spanish Influenza, AIDS, the Second World War, the Bay of Pigs Crisis and the 2004 Asian tsunami. Because they were so radically outside the norm, nobody had predicted them As you read this, you probably worry about paying the mortgage, what school your kids will go to, your retirement pension, whereas it's likely that, in the next ten years, something else will impact more on your life than any of these.

Ten years ago, you weren't worried that your home might fall into the sea because of climate change. If you don't live on the coast, you may still not be that worried, but your consciousness includes a serious concern about the fact that the ice caps are melting two decades faster than most scientists predicted just three years back: it's a black swan.

And even if climate change doesn't destroy your house, its financial effects (tax on carbon, tax on waste, increase cost of jet-fuel, home heating oil, petrol, diesel, increased cost of transport) will have a greater impact on your finances over the next decade than the mortgage rate you worried so much about, or the raise you fought so hard for.

Taking the mortgage as an example; global warming may have a bigger effect on your life than the single biggest purchase you ever made. Bet you spent a long time with a calculator before you bought the house. Bet you never factored in the ice caps. Black Swan.

Black Swans are easier to point to when they're negative. But they have just as big a positive effect on our lives. We meet our partners by chance because we went on holiday to some location to which there was a cheap flight. We become rich because we were in the home-buying business at the right time – just before the boom. Many companies are huge successes because of such luck. Consider Bill Gates. Wasn't he lucky to be a computer geek leaving college at exactly the time the silicon revolution happened? Imagine if he'd qualified as an accountant; think he'd be the richest man in the world?

'No no!' you cry. 'Bill's a genius and geniuses will always rise to the top.'

This is where Taleb is particularly interesting; he provides proof of how extreme success is often totally dependent on luck.

Let's say you look at a chart of the ten managed funds on sale through your stockbroker. Two of these funds have out-performed the others over the past three years. That must be proof that the guys in charge of them are good at their jobs. Right? Wrong.

The first mistake we tend to make is to look at too narrow a duration. Let's look at those funds over a decade. Now we see that only one fund has been successful for that long. Well, then, *that* fund's managers are the geniuses. Right? Wrong again.

The second mistake we make is to look at too narrow a catchment group. We should not look at the ten funds currently in operation. We should look at all the funds that have been available over that ten-year period. Now we might have as many as one hundred, ninety of which have failed and disappeared. Leaving us our ten. Out of which we have one genius. Right? Nope.

Look at it this way; let's say you put one hundred people in a room flipping coins. Each person will flip one hundred times. The chances that you will get ten heads in a row is one hundred to one. Which means that one person is statistically certain to get ten heads in a row. Does that mean he's a genius? Nope. Does he know something about coin tossing that the rest of us don't?

Nope. He just got lucky. So it is with fund managers, according to Taleb. And so it is with politicians, according to me.

If someone gets re-elected to their local council at every election for thirty years, the chances are that skill is in play. If someone gets to be Taoiseach, you can bet a lot of luck came into play. More luck than skill.

Imagine a job you can really apply for only if you're over forty-five and under sixty-seven. You can get the job only if you are in one of two parties. You can get returned for one of those parties only if someone in your constituency quits politics (or there's a bizarre upheaval). Then you'll be one of a few thousand seeking election. After that, you'll have to be elected party leader and that job interview only comes around once every five years (on average) so you've got four chances at the position.

While you wait you had better be in a constituency where your seat is assured, as failing to get elected at a general election puts you back to square one. You'll also have to hope no one else is in line for the job or your time will slide by while you wait for them to vacate. You then have to hope you're leader when your party gets to power (which if you're in Fine Gael means less than once a decade). And if you want longevity in the position you'll need to get elected during a period of economic stability and growth.

But skill could get you through all these obstacles, couldn't it? Nope. You obviously need to be skillful and competent but you also need to be lucky: Brian Cowen needed Bertie Ahern to get tired of being asked about his personal finances way back when; Bertie Ahern needed Albert Reynolds to put Harry Whelehan's foot in his mouth. Enda Kenny needed Michael Noonan's leadership to fail. Michael McDowell needed Mary Harney to get fed up being leader of the PDs and then Mary Harney needed a few hundred people in an affluent Dublin suburb to get fed up with Michael in order to put her back at the helm briefly before Ciaran Cannon needed Mary Harney to decide she was still fed up of being leader along with the advantage of their being fewer PDs in captivity than the bald eagle.

Whatever about bald eagles – that was Charles J. Haughey in his heyday – large-scale political success is riddled with black swans. Being in the right constituency, in the right party, at the right age, with the right friends and colleagues, with the right economic circumstances, at the right time. Those are the key deciding factors.

No politician wants to be told that. No business executive wants to be told it. No book-buyer wants to be told it. Because the thought that most of the factors influencing your future are not controllable is scary.

The publicity campaigns around successful politicians, or around the books written by business gurus, ignore the fact that three identical guys were unsuccessful because they didn't happen to have the right network or people or because they were there at the wrong time or because they weren't lucky enough. The perpetuation of the myth is greatly helped by the fact that the unsuccessful don't tend to arrive on TV programmes to face down the guru with the evidence that the unsuccessful guy did precisely the same as the guru claims to have done and is bankrupt.

Uncontrollable circumstances cause political failure. Unanticipated and ostensibly irrelevant issues can destroy a career or a government – remember Albert Reynolds's comment that it's not the big things that bring you down but the little things.

For the new politician, the biggest risk is forgetting about luck; each prime minister is shown to be the result of strategy, conspiracy and consummate skill. Very rarely do people assume that any of it was luck. This assumption of genius makes each previously successful leader a model for the next generation. When Bill Clinton was elected, all over Europe spin-doctors and politicians started to warble about the third way and, 'It's the economy, stupid.' When Blair was elected every press officer tried to make their leader do keepie-ups and play electric guitar. Every new politician is under pressure to ape the behaviour and strategy of whoever is flavour of the month up to that point.

Politicians and their handlers rarely learn the two most important things; first, the things the flavour of the month did worked for *him*, back *then*. And secondly, luck played a huge part. A *huge* part. The trick is to do everything to be prepared for the moment luck finds you.

That is particularly apposite for the politician who has come to politics after a successful and publicly recognised business career. This kind of background tends to make you buy into your own myth: the myth of control. 'I did this because I could,' the business success says. 'I was in charge. I was in control. I could buy and make and distribute a product or service.'

Great. The business executive, particularly if he or she has a high profile, then gets wooed by a political party and looking around at the currently elected members of that party, says to himself, 'Sure if a guy like your man with no teeth can get elected surely I can get elected.'

Then he discovers he can't. He may not get on the ticket. He may get on the ticket but not become one of the hundred and sixty-six guys who get in the front door of Leinster House. To stand watching an election count and find that your success and fame didn't carry you beyond the third count is devastating, not least because the focus of everybody's attention is on the people who *did* make it past the third count.

Many of the business people who don't make it into politics decide, as a result of their failure, that the whole political system is deeply flawed – how else could it not have embraced so obvious a talent? Few political rejects put the experience behind them without bitterness. It is a hell of an experience to have run a major business and then encounter the absolute lack of respect demonstrated by local gombeen men who rate a candidate only on their electability and whose instincts, honed on the hustings, can predict that electability with ruthless prescience.

Candidates parachuted from business often assume that they can bring the team and the capital they had in their business into this new arena. It rarely works. For them. It always works for the party. One of the great sadnesses of the business parachute candidate is that while they think they're professionalising what simpletons have done for years, their very candidacy can mean the simpletons are exploiting *them.*

If you're the director of elections, the one thing you have a lot of is candidates. The thing you've very little of is money. If you have a multimillionaire businessman on the ticket, you can be absolutely sure that for at least a year in advance of the election, that businessman will run the maximum allowable expenditure in his constituency and if he can pull it off, on the commuter routes into his constituency.

On top of that, by virtue of his fame in his previous life, he will get coverage. Tons of coverage. Media will love the notion of high-end business chap turning politician and high-end business chap is fairly guaranteed to assume that he will be Taoiseach within, say, a fortnight of his first election and will therefore talk high-end statesmanlike geopolitical guff (which media like) as opposed to discussing potholes and water rates (which media don't like).

The director of elections gets posters with the party name plastered all over them for free. Party leaflets for free. Party coverage in the national media for free. All of which benefits the party's other candidates in the constituency. The only requirement of the director of elections is to make vaguely empathetic noises when the candidate fails miserably.

Part of what will cause that failure is the tendency of candidates to assume that a fresh professional team is what's needed in the constituency, rather than working with the vagaries of the local organisation. That's a mistake.

The guys on the ground may be difficult but they know stuff no new team will be aware of. On the other hand, if you can create an alloy of your guys and the guys who used to be attached to the previous TD in the area and manage to get elected as a result, you must be sure to bind that team to you immediately thereafter. Because the seeds of the next election have already been sown and an experienced team of people around you who feel valued by you and enjoy helping you is invaluable.

Coming from business, new politicos tend to feel that it's not acceptable to ask people to do a professional job for nothing. These are the politicos who never last. Because they don't understand one of the most basic human needs, the one stressed more than a hundred years ago by William James: the need to be needed. The need to be appreciated. The need to belong to something special. The need to do something for which one is *not* paid, except in the unequalled coinage of someone else's esteem.

That same hunger for someone else's attention is one of the things new politicians on the canvass forget. They sometimes rate their success on a canvass by numbers reached and spoken to. It is, of course, important not to waste time on the canvass. People, when they encounter a politician they want to get rid of, tend to act in an indecisive way. Which is like bleeding into the water when you are running away from a shark.

'Oh Jeez,' they say, 'I'm not even sure I'll have time to make the polls.'

To the politician, this is an invitation to overwhelm a floating voter with enthusiasm. By the way, from the point of view of the person being canvassed, here's an infallible tip. The only way to get rid of a politician quickly is to greet them with wild enthusiasm, not vague discomfort.

'I am delighted to see you,' you say, grasping them warmly by the hand, 'because you are the man I am voting for. You have my number one.'

They'll be gone like a shot, delighted to know they have you in the bag and can go look for some undecideds to seduce.

Canvassing has to be the most mortifying experience in the world for any politician. You have to climb fences, push past wheelie bins and brave the family dog in order to reach the front door – only to be told to stick your leaflet. Or worse, depending on the mistakes the politician makes when the door is opened.

The first mistake is seeking someone who hasn't answered the door. When I was eighteen and could vote, I opened the front door to encounter a canvasser.

'Is your mother or father home?' she asked.

'Yes,' I said truthfully and closed the door.

The canvasser stood out there for about ten minutes. My feeling was: you asked the question, you got a truthful answer. Your problem was that you asked the wrong question. Your problem was that you insulted me with your assumption that I didn't have a vote and was therefore just a messenger boy.

There's more to that incident than the insult to a touchy teenager. (Not that I was a touchy teenager. Just a literal one.) Getting a vote is more than a matter of influencing the voter. Whether you are doing a campaign about environmental behaviour or health behaviour, one of the things that public relations people have noticed lately is that if you convince the kids the kids work on the parents.

If you have a fifteen- or seventeen-year-old on the door, who later says to his parents, 'Jasus your man came and he was respectful to me and he listened to what I had to say,' the parents will take the positive view, even if they weren't there.

'Fair dues to your man for taking the time with Junior,' they'll think. 'Because he didn't have to.'

You get the reflected glory.

The one thing you must *never* do, nor have any member of your support team do, is piss off either a potential voter or a relative of a potential voter. I remember once I pulled up at traffic lights and a woman canvassing for the European elections came up to me.

'Hi, I'm canvassing for so and so,' she said, proffering leaflets.

'Don't waste your time on me,' I told her, wanting to save her time. 'I am not going to vote.'

'Well that's not very responsible is it?' she answered. 'You have a civic duty to vote.'

'I take it back,' I said. 'I *am* going to vote and I am going to vote for everyone *except* your guy.'

Getting sanctimonious with a voter is never the way to go, even if the voter has provoked you. The first duty of a canvasser is to be like Mohammed Ali and do the rope-a-dope; lean back and let them punch you till they get tired. Remember, the most common complaint people make about politicians is that they don't listen. So your first duty is to disprove that. Stump up in front of them, greet them warmly, shake hands like a pro and, if necessary, let them work themselves tired giving out to you.

If there is anything concrete and doable within what they're saying, make it clear that you have listened, made a note and say you are going to come back to them about it. It's that simple. Just by showing patience, making a note and indicating openness, you can create the beginning of a relationship.

When call centres were originally set up, many of them had specific compensation for regular customer problems. Performance reviews speedily showed that some operators paid out less money than others in the form of compensation but had happier customers than the ones who had given more cash. What this pointed to was that if people felt their problem was fully *understood*, the compensation didn't matter so much.

If you complain about a fly in your carbonara and the waiter gruffly says he'll take it off the bill, you'll probably never eat in the restaurant again. If the waiter bursts into tears and indicates that he and the chef will go to Confession over this, you'll probably just eat the fly.

The Greek philosopher Seneca summed up the basic human need met by simply *attending:* 'Just listen to me for one minute,' he wrote. 'For one hour. For one day. Before I die in this wilderness of loneliness.'

FedEx are the arch exponents of this. A year ago, I had a package due from the United States. When it was two weeks late, I rang FedEx. A man named Brian told me the life story of my parcel. How it had dallied briefly in Memphis before travelling to Paris Charles de Gaulle, where a French baggage handler had put it on a jet to Dubai, rather than Dublin. At that point, my parcel was enjoying life in a sunny tax haven and wouldn't be returning for several weeks. Brian went on to explain how this not only brought shame on him but on Federal Express and possibly the nation of France. By the time we finished talking, I was no closer to getting my package but I was delighted to have met and talked to Brian and almost glad that my parcel had had a chance to see the world.

A former minister told me that it was this approach that got him elected. He maintained that he could see from fifty yards the expression that said 'Oh, here comes this pillock. I'm going to give him a piece of my mind.' He maintained that once he saw that expression, he knew he could win a vote. He'd not only take the piece of the mind but ask for the rest of it. He would let the voter beat him bloody on the doorstep and ask for more. 'I gave your man a good going over but he seems like a nice fella, actually,' is the unspoken reaction of the voter in this situation.

One TD made a canvassing career of his ability to listen and absorb the complaints handed to him at the doorstep. His technique was to carry a dictaphone. A dictaphone that had neither batteries nor a tape. When the constituent on the doorstep had fully vented their spleen he would pull the recorder out of his pocket and, in front of the spent constituent, dictate a letter.

> Letter to chief planning officer, re Mrs McDonagh's lamp-post [Remind me of the address, Mrs McDonagh?] outside 42 Main Street. Mrs McDonagh has now complained to the council [how many times again?] five times and has had no response. This is a disgrace and a failure of both duty and decency on your part. I demand that this problem be fixed post haste

or I will come to the council office and you will feel
my tongue in person. If there is any confusion about
what is required, you may call me at my constituency
office or call Mrs McDonagh directly [what is the
phone number here?] on 5556874. Yours etc.

The TD was then sure that if the lamp-post ever got repaired,
he got the credit and even if it didn't, Mrs McDonagh would tell
everyone she knew that he was a man of action who wrote a
fierce letter to the council on her behalf. Fundamentally, the Mrs
McDonaghs of his constituency watched him walk away from
their doorstep knowing (or at least believing) they had been
listened to. After that, it's a matter of getting and using their
name and actually asking for their vote. Asking for a vote and
getting them to confirm it to you is important. Getting someone
to verbally commit to something doesn't guarantee that they will
do it but it undoubtedly makes them more likely to do it.

Therefore, you ask for their number one and if they say they
won't give it to you, ask them to give you their second preference,
please. Most new candidates get so defeated when they can't
get a commitment to a first preference out of a voter that they
forget – if they ever understood – how vitally important third
or fourth preferences can be. Those preferences can take a
candidate through to the third count. If it's the candidate's first
time out, a respectable showing in a general election – a survival
to the third count with a reasonable number of votes – can make
all the difference when some sitting TD in that constituency
dies or resigns because of a scandal and the party has to select a
candidate. We have, in this country, an election system which is
brilliant but which only a handful of people fully understands.

Not many election systems will keep your vote working till it reaches old age and retires. Not many elections systems will let you decide: 'Well, if I don't get him I'll get her and if I can't get either of them, I can at least make sure I don't help *that* bastard.' It is a hell of a system. It prevents that first-past-the-post stuff you get in the US, with the inevitable and embittered binary opposition it generates. Of course, it has drawbacks. It does tend to create coalitions, to set up a mishmash of 'let's all be pals' governments.

In the US, in contrast, in the 2000 presidential election, George Bush got elected on perhaps 24 per cent of the popular vote. That means that more than 75 per cent of the nation did not vote for the man. They may not have voted against him but having to say that three out of four people didn't want you – that, in the literal sense of the word, they didn't bother their arse to go out and put you in to government – is an iffy way to lead a nation. If there was a proportional representation system in the US, you wouldn't have the vote split by Ralph Nader. Nader would have been eliminated and his votes counted back in and you would probably have had a different president who would have been more representative of the views of majority of Americans.

Ralph Nader ran in the hope of getting a certain percentage of the vote so that he would cross a major funding Rubicon for future elections. The problem from the Democratic point of view was that Gore needed just a little more than five hundred extra votes to win Florida and thereby the Presidency. Nader took a larger proportion of Democratic votes than Republican in that state: if he'd stayed at home, Gore would have received a few thousand more votes and become President. Nader has denied this, citing other swing states where he believes his campaign robbed votes from Republicans to the advantage of Al Gore.

The oddest part of the whole thing is that regardless of Nader splitting the vote, the nation which is so proud of its democracy returned George Bush when fewer people voted for him than Al Gore (the electoral college system allows a president to be returned when he hasn't won the popular vote. It happened with Benjamin Harrison in 1888 and Rutherford Hayes in 1876, both of whom got elected with fewer votes than their opponent.)

The remarkable thing is that we are able to say exactly what support Bush received. The US is a nation of over 300 million people. Yet (with the exception of anomalies like Ralph Nader) those who voted went either of two ways; Bush or Gore. It makes for an easy election to analyse and to predict; it's a binary choice: Republican or Democrat. And if more people go one way than the other, a president is elected. We have a tendency to view the Irish political system the same way; Fine Gael versus Fianna Fáil or Brian Cowen versus Enda Kenny. In reality, our governments are rarely elected in that kind of *mano-a-mano* titanic struggle. The 2007 election was won (and lost) as much by Labour and the Greens as by Enda Kenny and Bertie Ahern. It's a much more challenging result to analyse and predict than the US result.

One of the unusual aspects of the 2007 general election was the presence of Frank Luntz on RTÉ. Luntz is a political pollster from the US who put forward theories and notions at great length about the various parties and their leaders. When the election count came around, he broke off from explaining how in being wrong he had been right, to announce that one of the most fascinating experiences for him in coming to Ireland was watching our count system in action. Then he said he had been watching it for four hours and still didn't understand it. How a man can predict the operations of a system he doesn't understand is intriguing.

The credibility of Frank Luntz's work in the Irish general election of 2007 can probably be further called into question when you look at the results he came up with: he found that Bertie Ahern and Pat Rabbitte were gifted and popular politicians, whereas Enda Kenny was more or less useless. Less than twelve months after Frank's pronouncement, Enda Kenny was the only one still in a job. In the Irish context, you have to feel a little sorry for Frank.

Niels Bohr once said, 'If quantum mechanics hasn't profoundly shocked you, you haven't understood it yet.' The same is true of proportional representation. At some point in the human genome project they will isolate the chromosome that allows one to comprehend the system. It seems to run in families. Usually rural families. To those who understand, it is like breathing or walking: it requires no thought, they just see the patterns. The rest of us, it makes our noses bleed by the time we get to count four.

I was asked to attend an IFA (Irish Farmers' Association) election count many years ago. The count was to last for six hours. During the second hour a man with few teeth and less hair came up to me and announced the winner, his margin of victory, the number of counts yet to come and the time the victory would be announced. I asked him how he knew. He gave me a look indicating that such a stupid question proved all his darkest suspicions about Dubliners, stuck his little pencil behind one of his large ears and strode off. He was, of course, completely right in all his predictions.

Proportional representation allows one man one vote to become real. I once watched a county councillor read count reports. 'My man's made it to count three,' he announced with some pride. 'I gave him a third preference to help him through.

There it is. *There.*' He handed me the newspaper which said his man had made it to that count by one single transfer. Not many systems allow a voter to see their vote working in the following day's papers. For a new candidate, that adds a subtlety that doesn't exist in the UK or in America. It adds an air of unpredictability and a layer of disassociation from what happens at national level.

An election, a political career, a government, can hang on the decisions of three hundred people. Therefore if you want to win that election, build that career or be in that government, you need to exploit every piece of luck that comes your way – in addition to doing the skill, competence and diligence bits.

The big question for new political candidates is not what type of politician they'll be, nor even whether or not they'll get elected. It's why anyone in their right mind would want to be elected in the first place.

The science fiction writer Isaac Asimov wrote a short story about a man who wakes up to a piece of unspecified bad news. Having told his family, he looks out his window and finds the street littered with television broadcast trucks, journalists and three large black limousines. The twist in the story comes towards the end. It's predicated on a future where the state has educated everyone to a level where they could be president, culled anyone who actually *wants* the job as mentally unstable and thereafter appoints every president as the result of a lottery. This man's piece of bad news is that for the next four years he has to run the nation.

Being a politician is a rotten job. You have no security of tenure. The EU working time directive doesn't apply to you. Everyone believes they own you and should have free access to you. You're pilloried, constantly. And forgotten, quickly. You work in the Dáil, in the car, in the pub, at dinner, at home, in your clinic, every hour you are awake. There's no guarantee that, no matter how hard you work, your customers will give you your job back. And the more senior you are, the worse it gets. Winston Churchill saved Britain and possibly the wider world from Nazism. At least, that's what the people of Britain thought, after the Second World War. It didn't stop them immediately turfing him out of office.

Whether you personally liked him or not, Bertie Ahern was Ireland's best Taoiseach ever, by almost any objective measure you could apply. His tenure saw our longest period of sustained economic growth, the biggest developments in our health system, saw peace break out and provided stable governmental coalitions as well as creating almost total employment. He was also the second-longest-serving Taoiseach in our history. And within three months of his resignation he was forgotten. Not literally, but as a figure of national importance.

That kind of amnesia seldom happens outside politics. In the private sector a successful chief executive can expect not only a golden handshake but several years of consultancy and board memberships. In politics, your resignation speech and epitaph are one and the same.

Bertie Ahern called a press conference on 2 April 2008 to announce his departure from office. Before he and his cabinet had walked back up the steps of Government Buildings the public debate had begun about who would follow him and whether or not there would be a leadership election.

As hurtful as that might have been to Bertie Ahern, it is the constant reality of politics.

The first thing that a new politician should learn about voters is that They Almost Never say Thanks.

3

THE MYTH OF LEADERSHIP

When you think about it, Churchill had it easy. He didn't have television to cope with and he had a war which put him in almost complete control of the media, a war into which the British people had bought. All he had to do was make with the rhetoric. Which he did. In the process, he left a race-memory among political aficionados to the effect that leadership is essentially a matter of rhetoric.

In Irish politics, you'll hear older TDs talking about celebrated individuals from the past as having been wonderful orators and brilliant speakers. Their nostalgia for the magnificence of the old 'Bell, book and candle' rhetoric ignores the reality, which is that television has taken a lot of the value out of it, by virtue of its emphasis on the immediate and the concrete. If it won't fit in a soundbite, television cannot cope with it, except in late-night minority Dáil Report programmes, which attract only political nerds anyway. If television doesn't include it, then print media will not devote much space to it. Print media throughout the western world spend much less space than they used to on parliamentary speeches and debate. As a direct result, no longer do many TDs bother to try to impress the public gallery or the press gallery or the opposition or their own lads with their speeches. Oratory is not at a premium in politics these days.

Nor do political leaders do much in the way of quick repartee, even insulting repartee, like the famous exchange between Lady Astor and Winston Churchill, where she told him that if she was his wife, she'd put arsenic in his breakfast cup of tea and he retorted that if he was her husband, he'd drink it.

Some of the most successful Irish political leaders never did quick repartee. Charlie Haughey did off-the-record profanity. Bertie Ahern did impatient snappishness ('You're only a waffler' or 'Are you deaf, as well as stupid?') Pat Rabbitte's ad libs had the precision of advance preparation, although even doing his homework didn't save him from the backlash that hit him during the general election when he described Michael McDowell as 'a menopausal Paris Hilton'.

The fact is that oratorical genius and instant wit are not pre-requisites for leadership, although the former may be essential during wartime. General Patton was the American who led the single most successful campaign in the history of warfare and famously came to the rescue of the 101st Airborne in Bastogne at the culmination of the Ardennes offensive ('Battle of the Bulge') in the closing months of the Second World War. Patton was a brilliant military commander but he's now probably remembered more for his oratory than for his tactics. He believed that one of the key tasks for a leader was to look and act like a leader:

> People ask me why I swagger, swear, wear flashy uniforms and sometimes two pistols. The press and others have built a picture of me. So, now, no matter how tired or discouraged, or really ill I may be, if I don't live up to that picture, my men are going to say, 'The old man's had it. The old son-of-a-bitch has had it.' Then their own confidence, their own morale will take a big dip.

As well as wearing the flashy uniforms and the ivory-handled Colt .45 and .357 Magnum, Patton developed an oratorical style designed to fit the 'old-blood-and-guts' image. Addressing his troops before D-Day, Patton delivered a speech laden with expletives and gore:

> We'll win this war but we'll win it only by fighting and by showing the Germans that we've got more guts than they have; or ever will have. We're not going to just shoot the sons-of-bitches, we're going to rip out their living Goddamned guts and use them to grease the treads of our tanks. We're going to murder those lousy Hun cocksuckers by the bushel-fucking-basket. War is a bloody, killing business. You've got to spill their blood, or they will spill yours. Rip them up the belly. Shoot them in the guts. When shells are hitting all around you and you wipe the dirt off your face and realise that instead of dirt it's the blood and guts of what once was your best friend beside you, you'll know what to do!

Patton explained this approach thus:

> When I want my men to remember something important, to really make it stick, I give it to them double dirty. It may not sound nice to some bunch of little old ladies at an afternoon tea party but it helps my soldiers to remember. You can't run an army without profanity; and it has to be eloquent profanity. An army without profanity couldn't fight its way out of a piss-soaked paper bag.

Patton's recent popularity as a management and leadership poster-boy had two effects. The first effect was on business people. Managers have taken to quoting Patton totally out of context. 'May God have mercy on our enemies in the sprocket and grommet market, because in the first quarter of 2009; we won't! ' They do this because they think grommet sales are directly linked to their capacity to inspire and lead their sales teams. This is (to echo Patton) bullshit.

The second effect of Patton's popularity has been a growing belief that leaders are meant to look and act like leaders. Politicians are under constant pressure to look like statesmen. This somewhat ignores a long history of leaders who looked far from statesmanlike: Napoleon was a squirt; Nelson was effeminate; Churchill was short, fat and bald; Disraeli looked and smelled (we are told) like an old tart and George Washington had wooden teeth.

Good looks are great. But they're extras. Handy to have. A politician can become a leader without either. Being ugly as sin isn't helpful in any walk of life but you don't have to look like George Clooney to become leader of a political party. A politician can become a leader without any showy stuff.

There's a line in a movie which is the film version of the book *We Were Soldiers Once and Young* by Lt. General Harold T. Moore. He was the man who led Custer's Brigade, the 7th cavalry, in the first pitched battle in Vietnam. In the movie version, Moore had an ex-Second World War paratrooper as his sergeant major. In the film, as in reality, Moore was a young, highly-educated colonel with this grisly old sergeant major. They're all kitting up for the conflict, when one of the young soldiers talks to the sergeant major.

'Are you not going to get an M16?' the young soldier asks,

because all the sergeant major has is his pistol.

'By the time I need to start shooting,' the older soldier responds, 'there's going to be lots of them lying around.'

You get the sense from really old-school politicians, particularly the ones who aren't at the very front of things, like Enda Kenny until he got the leadership of Fine Gael, that they walk around with a pistol knowing there will be a lot of M16s lying around by the time they need to start shooting. They know the way everything functions. They know how all the debates work and what you have to show up for and what you don't have to show up for. They've got a sharp instinct for what you get your knickers in a bunch over and what you don't. They are collegial with everyone in the Dáil or at least the vast majority of the TDs. They've long ago got not cynical but practical.

Long before James Carville articulated the notion of the continuing campaign, these older politicians know what younger arrivals don't: that from the moment they first set foot in Leinster House, they should be deciding first and foremost how they're going to get back in five years. Your reason for being there is to get re-elected. That's what democracy is. You want your job back.

You certainly don't want to buy into any of the myths of leadership. Not then. Not ever. If you go along the shelves of business books in any bookshop, you find them divided into two kinds. About two-thirds of them are modern and business-based, so you have Bill Gates or Richard Branson telling how they did it. The other third are historical and what's significant is that most of them relate to warfare. Alexander. Attila. Sun Tzu. Machiavelli. Because most of them assume a chronic circumstance of war, they concentrate on the capacities a leader requires in order to defeat the enemy and lead his people towards a brighter, richer future. The *liebensraum* concept was not confined to Hitler.

The difficulty with most of these books is they assume the presence of an enemy and the possibility of a better world. Enemies are easy to find in business. Few companies exist without competition and fixation on that competition has given impetus to some of the most successful companies in history. Nike operated for many years under the mission statement 'Crush Reebok'; Honda went with 'We will crush, squash and slaughter Yamaha.' In the corporate world, getting your constituents to sign up to vanquish an enemy is relatively easy, because that vanquishing is directly linked to each constituent's pay cheque. If I work as a tappet-polisher in Honda and Honda squashes Yamaha, then my team will have to make twice as many tappets. I get promoted and the kids get the big-screen TV they've been nagging me about.

It doesn't work so easily for political parties. If Fianna Fáil brought out an election manifesto entitled, 'We will dine on the entrails of Fine Gael,' they'd get great media coverage, motivate the grassroots immensely but gain very little traction with the average punter, who's probably more concerned with the rats in his kid's school than with the consumption of Richard Bruton's duodenum. For a politician to motivate the electorate against an enemy requires war. Real war. With guns. And dead people. This is an option for some politicians. The US and Russian presidents can have the odd geopolitical scuffle to motivate the lads at home and the British can occasionally dabble in peasant-bombing to gain a few votes (think Vulcan bombers hitting a field in Argentina or the SAS marching into Iraq). It's not a real option for an Irish politician. Declaring war on the Isle of Man would only serve to confuse the electorate and give the Defence

Forces Chief-of-Staff, Major General Dermot Earley, a hernia.

Without enemies to aim at, politicians are forced to go with the 'better-world' approach: Kennedy pointing to the moon, Roosevelt promising a New Deal, Clinton describing the Third Way and Tony Blair bouncing around to D:Ream's 'Things Can Only Get Better'. That's all grand if things are bad. A recession. Better yet, a depression. Hyper-inflation. Urban unrest. Union agitation. Student riots. But none of these was the case in recent Irish election campaigns.

If the students are stoned, the unions benchmarked, inflation pegged at 2.5 per cent and there's total employment it's awful hard to give the better-world speech. Hence recent Irish general elections were filled with notions about 'being more than an economy' and 'building communities' and other such well-meaning platitudes that the electorate looked at and thought, 'Yeah, communities are important. I must buy a bigger house in a nicer community.'

Elections in prosperous times are boring for the media, difficult for politicians and irrelevant to the public. Good times are when newspapers write worried editorials about voter apathy. Of course the voters are apathetic. If things are good, why would they bother listening to a whole bunch of politicians telling them that they will make them continue to be good except they'll flavour them with cinnamon.

Voters are asked by journalists, 'What do you think the issues are for this election?' Answer: health, crime and the economy. Here's a rule of thumb; if voters list election issues that exactly overlap with government departments designed to be responsible for those issues, then there are no issues. Issues are singular, specific and present tense, not plural, non-specific and future tense. It's like the difference between the warnings on cigarette packs and Superglue tubes. The cigarette packs give you the general, non-specific and future tense; these things *might* give you cancer or heart disease or erectile dysfunction (but not just yet). Superglue gives the singular, specific and short-term warning; get this stuff on your fingers and it'll stick 'em together (right now). So it is with electoral issues: 'My kid can't get a job.'; 'I was assaulted and the man walked free.'; 'I've had to call the Vincent de Paul to help me get enough money to feed my family.' Singular. Personal. Now. They're the kind of problems that have many owners; the Gardaí, the community, the education system, consultants, private hospitals, politicians, the Church. Once people start saying they're 'concerned about crime' or think 'the health system is in a shambles' or they're 'worried about the economy' you know the problems are abstract and general, not real and specific.

The clearest demonstration of this in action is the difference between the national focus in the year before the 2007 election and in the year after it. Before the 2007 election we were told by poll after poll that the themes of national concern were crime, quality of life and the health service, all under the overarching theme of the economy. They were all broad, non-specific 'issues'. Seven months after the election, crime, health and quality of life had disappeared from the national agenda because the economy theme had moved from broad and vague to narrow and specific and in doing so, sucked the oxygen from every other potential concern. By the start of 2008 the discussion about the economy was no longer well-meaning platitudes about 'growth' and 'competitiveness'. It had become personal. It was: 'Is my job secure?' or 'Will I end up taking a pay cut?' or 'Will I lose my house?' or 'Will I be able to pay my debts?' or 'Can I afford fuel, car tax, home heating, groceries?'

This kind of national discussion is fertile ground for political parties. They get to debate something that affects nearly every member of the electorate in a real, current and pressing way. And for the opposition, even if the economy recovers before the next election, the recession of 2008 will radically change the playing field for that next election.

When the analysts looked at the opinion polls in the lead-up to the 2007 election, they said that Fianna Fáil had 'gained traction' in the last week and had swayed enough people to keep them in power. This is simply wrong. For two reasons:

First you always have to question *post-factum* rationalisations of strategy. If someone from Fianna Fáil had – in advance of the last week of the campaign – mentioned that it was their intent to do a big final push and that they had a plan to deliver a swing, then it might be believable, but political campaigns are breeding grounds for *post-factum* rationalisations. It's like being a witch-doctor; you put feathers in your hair and dance around, hoping that it will eventually rain. When it does you point to the feathers and dancing and say, 'See, I told yis; it was all me that caused that.' Then you wait for the tributes and respect to flow in your direction.

The second reason is because the change in polled view towards the dying days of the last election was predictable. It's the 'her-indoors' principle. The world, and Ireland in particular, is full of pubs and sports clubs in which people give out about their spouses. They talk about how they're sick of the person they're married to. They pick at their faults and wait for their friends to tell them they could have done better. The most extreme version I've seen was a group of guys discussing a man they knew who had just been released after doing eighteen years in Mountjoy for killing his wife. One of the group stared into space for a while, then announced wistfully, 'I'm married twenty-one years. If I'd killed her at the outset, I'd be out by now.'

Lots of people in that group may have decided that he had a grossly dysfunctional relationship with his wife but none of them read his statements as genuine intent to commit murder. Similarly most spouses who declare, 'One of these days I'll leave him or her,' don't actually do it.

That was the dynamic before the 2007 election. A lot of voters expressed disgruntlement with the Fianna Fáil government. They sat in the metaphorical pub and declared they were going to go home and throw the ring back at them. But there's a big difference between declaring that kind of intent and actually getting divorced. Hence the swing in the polls. In the last week, disgruntled threat had either to disappear or become definite action. And a significant number of people decided not to sign the divorce papers.

They did it for a really good reason: the economy. Ireland's economic success was intrinsically linked to Fianna Fáil. Few could say how, but it had happened under their governance and only under their governance so there had to be cause and effect. Before the last election Fianna Fáil was able to say to the electorate, in effect, 'Ah, you wouldn't hit me with the economic baby in me arms?' And they were right.

Since then, cause has separated from effect. The economy has nose-dived straight down the loo. It may claw its way back out, but even if it does, Fianna Fáil will no longer be able to use it as a shield against attack.

Fianna Fáil compounded that weakened position with a number of post-election fumbles uncharacteristic of the party in recent years. First they appointed a leader without an election. For Cowen this was, in theory, wonderful. It may prove not to be so. On of my colleagues wrote a feature, when Cowen was appointed, questioning the advisedness of taking a position like party leader and Taoiseach without an election. His argument drew heavily on one of Machiavelli's principles:

> It is to be remarked that, in seizing a state, the usurper ought to examine closely all those injuries that it is necessary for him to inflict. He should carry them out all at once so as not to have to repeat them daily. In this way, by not continually unsettling men, he will be able to reassure them, and win them to himself by benefits. He who does otherwise, either from timidity or evil advice, is always compelled to keep the knife in his hand. He can neither rely on his subjects, nor can they bind themselves to him, owing to their continued and repeated wrongs. Injuries ought to be done all at one time, so that, being tasted less, they offend less. Benefits ought to be given little by little, so that the flavour of them may last longer.

In Cowen's case, the knife may need to be ever in the hand for a simple reason. If a leader is elected and then the party wants a change of leader, a number of people will have to accept that they made a bad choice. If a leader is appointed without being elected, it is much easier for dissatisfaction to coalesce around people who can mutter, 'Well, I never voted for him.'

The choice of Cowen may prove to be a fumble in itself (he was one of the best *gauliters* or *consiglieris* a leader could wish for but gauliters and consiglieris rarely make good bosses) although that is yet to be seen. The fumble that is definite and measurable is the government's handling of the ESRI's declaration of recession.

It was one of the rare instances where the national need for leadership moved from myth to reality; a new Taoiseach, a new Minister for Finance, new coalition partners and a recession. A confluence of factors that screamed for a man-with-a-plan. And a confluence of factors that provided the perfect opportunity for the new Taoiseach to cement his position. With four years to go before the next election (although that may shorten) it mattered little what the plan was. It also mattered little if the plan annoyed voters, in fact it mattered little if the plan worked; so much time would have passed by the next election that any offence could be well forgiven and any failings could be remedied. What mattered was that the Taoiseach was seen to be in charge. This was not the perception that was left with the nation.

The time between now and the next election may see a consolidation of Cowen's position and the end of our economic problems. Counter-intuitively that may make it a harder election for everyone to fight than if there were chunky, specific problems to deal with.

If you're a politician in an issue-free period you have serious problems. Your job is just as much on the line as it is in a crisis but it's way more difficult to predict how to protect it. In the last (2007) Irish general election, the electorate was bored with Fianna Fáil (but not bored enough to put Fine Gael into power). That's it. No fancier than that. An industry exists to interpret why the electorate makes the decisions it does and it would collapse if it just said: 'They got a bit fed up with the guys they had but thought the other lads weren't great either.' But it's the reality.

In that kind of election the politician is better off spending his time thinking about local delivery than dreaming about the nation's future.

4

The Myth of Power

In order to deliver certain things to your constituency and to your local activists, the first step to leadership helps: getting a job as a front-bench spokesperson. In such a job, you're in a better position to be able to deliver those things.

But what many younger politicians don't realise is that every promotion, whether within a government or an opposition party, gives you only marginal extra power, while it *enormously* increases the demand, back in your constituency, for the delivery of concrete results. The politicians who don't get re-elected tend to be the ones who never get a handle on that delicate balance. They lose touch with local realities.

The toughest thing the newly-elected politician has to do is become a decent parliamentarian and legislator while doing this in a way that doesn't prevent them doing anything else. Some politicians completely ignore the requirement to be a parliamentarian/legislator, instead constantly screaming for attention for their own areas, whether these be Kerry, Mayo Waterford or Offaly. This approach breaches all the material taught in university political science courses, because it effectively ignores the central function for which TDs are elected. But let's be clear about two realities. This approach gets a considerable minority of TDs of all parties re-elected, one election after another, down through the decades. And it isn't easy. You have to batter on about your local constituency unendingly. You have to do every clinic that's going. You have to send out your newsletter around the area. You have to go on local radio several times a week and appear in the local newspaper week in, week out. In addition, you have to go to every funeral in the constituency.

This approach basically requires that the TD treat himself or herself like a posher local councillor. They become the go-to guy or gal. It's hard to do that and maintain a political career where you're trying to be a spokesman on certain issues. The task of an opposition spokesperson is made difficult by the fact that they do not have access to a rake of civil servants, although it is made easier by the possibility of fierce, high-profile opportunistic response to anything the government does which makes people fed up. (For government backbenchers, not being able to do this without infuriating the party whip and the party leader is a constant nagging frustration.)

That's the key thing people most misunderstand about politicians. Being a politician is about as hard a job as a human being can have. Politicians have to work harder than almost anybody else. Their day has no boundaries – if there's a committee meeting scheduled at 7.00, if someone has a delegation arriving at 7.15, you have to cope with both. People want you for lunch, they want you for coffee, they just want to meet you. You've got committee work, you've got to appear in the Dáil, you have to do the lunchtime news, you have to go on to the afternoon broadcast.

After that, there's a presentation from a lobby group or an exhibition at which you have to 'say a few words' or there's some event like the ploughing championships that you can't afford not to turn up at. You have to do all that before you go to dinner with someone who has a cunning plan they want you to support and at 10.00 pm you finally drag your sorry ass home. You do that all week and then you get to travel down to your constituency, try and mind your constituency office, be nice to the person who has been answering all the phones, get back to the key people who have rung you, who have emailed you, who have faxed you. You do all that, you manage to drag yourself to bed, you get up again the next morning and you go and sit in a pub for six hours while people complain at you.

It's just a terrible job and at the end of doing that for what feels like a lifetime you walk around every house in your area and beg them for your job while they give out to you. Under certain international conventions most of what politicians have to do to stay employed is illegal. Imagine a potential employer seeking to recruit a bright, ambitious, well-educated person on these terms:

> We're offering you a job at €90,000 a year. You're going to have to come in whenever we feel like calling you in, on whatever day we feel like, leave whenever we say, come back from an overseas trip if we demand it, meet whomever we choose to have you meet. We can't guarantee that the job will last any specific time or that you'll get it back once the contract ends. People are going to give out to you a lot and say horrible things about you in the media. Best of luck.

In the commercial world, a job applicant would walk without a second thought. In politics, candidates stay. Politics at every level, individually and collectively, is the triumph of hope over experience. When someone wants to get into politics, you could give them a month's intensive tutorial in the horrible realities they will face and establish for them without the shadow of a doubt that it's a terrible job and they will still want to put themselves on the ticket. You do get lifetime parking at Leinster House. I actually do believe there are people who run for TD just for the parking.

There are exceptions to all that I have said. Charlie McCreevy not only did very little constituency work, he did practically no canvassing when the general election came around, yet he got elected because he was such a unique – and uniquely-appealing – figure. However, the pressure in the political market is building all the time, so the chances are small that the next few years will throw up a Charlie McCreevy, who effectively says, 'Elect me if you want me. Don't if you don't,' and gets away with it. (Of course it helped that he was Minister for Finance throughout most of the years of economic growth.)

New TDs in one of the smaller government parties (now that single-party government is a nostalgic memory of the distant past) assume that their lives are going to be exciting and positive because their party is in power. The reverse is the case. For starters, they are held responsible for everything negative. In addition, it's going to be harder to be promoted than if they were backbenchers in the opposition. It's much easier to change around the front bench if you are an opposition leader than if you are the Taoiseach. When the Taoiseach decides to do a cabinet reshuffle, it means that ministers are going to lose their jobs, together with the perks and the prestige that go with those jobs. The humiliation is enormous, because, even if the Taoiseach explains both to the ousted minister and to the media that the minister has performed superbly but for a long period and it's time to give others a chance, the newspaper headline will inevitably use a word like 'Fired' and, as you get behind the wheel of a car, not having had to drive yourself for years, you do so with a sense of personal rejection and mortification.

Because any reasonably sensitive leader knows this, he or she is likely to postpone cabinet reshuffles until they become inescapable. Bertie Ahern was constantly under media attack for his failure to refresh his cabinets. But he had a team – not of close personal friends but of men and women who knew precisely how much they owed him. In addition to the loyalty factor this generates, there is the accompanying advantage that each member of the cabinet knew how every other member thought, which does tend to streamline the process of legislating.

All this means that if you are an opposition backbencher, you have more scope for promotion than if you are a member of a government party. That's the advantage. The disadvantage is that the promotion, when it comes, is not as rewarding as being appointed a minister or a minister of state. A spokespersonship on the opposition benches can be a lot of fun, though, and provide an ambitious and diligent TD with a great opportunity to learn, not only how to be an effective Dáil debater but also how all the civil and public service systems work. Which means that if the spokesperson eventually gets into power, they are going to be competent and authoritative much sooner than if they had been on the government backbenches for several years.

What makes the boredom on the government backbenches just about bearable is the fact that, whether or not you actually have it, you are able to claim to your constituents that you have access to ministers.

'Leave it with me,' you say. 'I'll have a word later tonight with Minister X.' You can then come back and quote the minister's immediate reaction and future plans on the issue. There's that sense of access among the government backbenchers that you don't have if you're in the opposition.

The first element of meritocracy within the Dáil is on the opposition backbenches. Look at Fergus O'Dowd's performance for Fine Gael before the last election. He dug stuff up himself. He talked to people. He developed relationships. He got on top of issues and he broke major stories and scandals in collaboration with selected media outlets. He managed to achieve all that, while operating from the Fine Gael's backbenches.

There is the scope and the time if you're an opposition backbencher in a way that is similar to journalism. Good investigative journalists know that by building relationships with people in their area of specialism they get a sniff of the wind of what's going on. The same is true for backbenchers. They should be building relationships and getting feeds from various organisations and individuals in their area that they can then use on the floor of the Dáil. That's when you ultimately begin to make a name for yourself.

But make sure it's not the wrong sort of name. Try not to do the big hero, where you end up getting yourself slapped down in front of the whole country. When Michael McDowell was Minister for Justice, one opposition spokesperson got at him and provoked the senior counsel, red in tooth and claw, to retaliate. McDowell disassembled him across the floor of the Dáil. Every now and then you still get that great moment of debate particularly when a young hotshot takes on the seasoned hand on the far side of the house. Everyone just sort of covers their eyes and thinks, 'Oh no, son, why did you do that?'

To which the short answer usually is, 'Because I was encouraged by the media.' The media encourage backbenchers, particularly maverick backbenchers, to do all the things that will ruin their career. What the media want in a backbencher is someone who is half-way between Robin Williams and Charles Manson. Witty as hell but leaving blood on the floor.

They're looking for people who will 'speak their mind'. Now, the one thing you know is that when someone says, 'I'm the sort of fella who tells it like it is,' or, 'I always speak my mind,' his mind is always negative and what he says always takes the form of a personal attack. When a backbencher does that, he or she gets great column inches. 'Oh isn't she a breath of fresh air,' say the journalists, noting the soundbites. 'She shoots from the hip, she tells it like it is.' While several of the backbencher's party colleagues think, 'Yeah, that's because she's lazy and clueless and good for nothing but mouthing.'

The attention of the media, however, can cause the aforesaid maverick backbencher to morph into something much more dangerous. Suddenly they are not only appearing and being quoted in newspapers but lauded in opinion columns and editorials as 'full of courage and fresh thinking'. They're like a dog that gets a biscuit and a scratch behind the ears when they stand on their hind legs. Rewarded by attention, they keep doing it and doing it until eventually they put their foot so squarely in their mouth they get fired or their electorate says, 'God, she's a gobshite. How did we miss that?' And once the electorate cop on to *that*, the politician doesn't get re-elected. The only way you can safely continue to behave in this pointless reckless way is if you're an independent TD, in which case the rules about gobshites are more lax. If you're an independent TD you're almost definitely there to deliver for one constituency a series of specific things and as long as you can batter on about them you can pretty much set fire to your shoes the rest of the time.

Any fool can manage success. It takes a genius to manage

failure and that's what Fianna Fáil has been doing for the last twenty years. They've gone from the position they held under Jack Lynch, where they had a majority so overwhelming (in the 1977 general election) that it made the entire opposition look like a boutique shop selling stools up against Ikea. Instead of going through a grieving process about the loss of the prospect of single-party government, they've done a Baileys. The theory about Baileys goes that Baileys Irish Cream many years ago decided that while they had started off as a semi-niche player in the market there was a risk that someone else was going to come in with something new and funky like puréed leprechaun à la rum which would eat into their market share. So they created Sheridans. What Sheridans did, particularly in the early years, was to create a barrier to entry for any other similar product.

If Fianna Fáil had done it deliberately, it would have been ingenious to create the PDs. The PDs were the Sheridans to Fianna Fáil's Baileys. There was no barrier to entry into that end of the slightly posher Fianna Fáil market, while Fianna Fáil, which should in theory hate the Progressive Democrats forever, regarded them as that most delightful of assets, the dispensable ally: 'When you're with us, that'll be grand and when things finally go bad, it is you who'll get lynched and buried – the few of you that are left, not us.'

These days Fianna Fáil goes into coalition with one party, then two parties, in a rolling erosion pattern whereby Fianna Fáil is the continuation party, the cherry-picker party and all others get seduced into coalition, then blamed for what goes wrong and go back to opposition weakened. In some cases, terminally weakened. Look at the PDs. Although they never did go back to opposition; they were too useful to Fianna Fáil in government.

5

The Myth of the Ministerial Car

The great advantage of being the Continuity Fianna Fáil party is that there's no learning curve at cabinet. Ministers are either experienced at being ministers or they're experienced at being ministers of state or their father was a minister, so they know the ropes. A small party going into government with them has an awful problem in this regard. They have to run to catch up, just to understand procedures and protocols. They're suspicious of Fianna Fáil putting one over on them. Their own supporters want them to achieve wonders within an impossibly short period of time. And they have to come to terms with the permanent government: the civil service.

New ministers should really treat their civil servants the way you would if you were a dog entering a new pack. Find whoever appears to be the alpha male and flip him on to his back. Because you have to establish who's in charge and if you don't do it in the first few days, you'll never do it. An awful lot of ministers are run by their civil servants. The weak, the vacillating, the nice, the odd and the thoughtful all end up 'going native', absorbing through their pores the thinking of their principal officers and assistant secretary generals.

The civil service mandarins can spot such a minister a mile off. They love that kind. (The kind of minister who is cordially loathed by the Civil Service is the rude, inattentive person who won't read the documents handed to him or her, understands nothing of how things actually happen within a big system and spends about ten minutes a week in the department because he or she would much prefer to be out in RTÉ or swanning around Leinster House meeting delegations.)

The civil service doesn't like intemperate action men or action women. They prefer the kind of minister who can be handed a policy document and put in a room to read it and consider the strategic implications of it, allowing everyone in the department to go off and do stuff or not do stuff as the case may be. The civil service prefer clever well-informed ministers to stupid ones but they like their ministers biddable. They particularly like ministers who allow their diaries to be managed. Really political ministers never do. They're always opportunistic and responsive, driving a hole through a neatly-prescribed schedule as circumstances demand. It drives the civil servants nuts.

The worst time, for a good senior civil servant – the man or woman who has stayed in the public sector because they think what they do is important – is the week after a general election, when it becomes clear that they're not going to get the same minister back. Each department worries in a different way. The guys in Education over in Marlborough Street consider the possibility of getting someone who was only recently dragged out of a primary school where they were a teacher, eager to tell them how to run educational policy for the entire nation. The ones in the ghastly glass tower where they keep the Department of Health are fearful of getting someone who thinks buying beds will solve all the problems of the health system and who'll be intimidated by the first hospital consultant they meet.

In the Custom House, they're always pretty sanguine, not

least because so much environmental policy is set by Europe and can't be contravened by a new minister.

The relationship that the new minister builds with the civil servants in the department is important because the biggest mistake you can make is going to war with your own Department. There's no point in doing that because there's more of them than there is of you and they've more experience at it. They'll just wrap you up in detail and you'll never get anything done.

When new ministers go in on their first day, traditionally what has happened is that they are welcomed by the top bods and handed a huge green folder, held together at the top by a string with a metal post on each end, which contains hundreds of pages of briefing materials. If it's a big department, new ministers may find themselves clutching four or five such folders, each replete with detail the new person will never come to terms with.

I'm not sure that system is the best one. It cuts across what we know about how people learn. It might be much more productive to have sessions at which the new minister asks questions, arising from which the folders of information are drawn up, not filled with general guff but with the information that particular minister needs at that particular time.

Civil servants produce reading material in volume. Politicians don't read it. Some politicians do. Of course they do. The ministers who read everything cover-to-cover and could quote from page 76 include Alan Dukes, Noel Dempsey, Gemma Hussey and Pádraig Flynn. I won't name the guys who don't do their homework at all, winging it at cabinet meetings when one of their colleagues queries the data on which the assumption stated in paragraph 14 is based.

The line of tension between ministers and civil servants about the production and reading of documentation is a constant.

It never improves but sometimes it worsens, when given ministers become overwhelmed and resentful at the amount of documentation being handed to them to take home at the weekend when they'd rather go golfing. Albert Reynolds, the Taoiseach who effectively carried through the northern peace process, is sometimes referred to as 'the one page man' because he once told a civil servant that he didn't want a complete folder of data. The key points should, he stated, be put on one page.

Apparently Eisenhower took the same approach. When you're in overall command of armies from America, Britain, France and elsewhere, you can't afford the time to read lengthy notes when a more junior officer can go through the material, select what requires decisions and make recommendations.

Picking your ministry is not within your competence, which is just as well, since everybody wants Finance because of the myth that you can never become Taoiseach without experience in an economic department. At any given time, one particular department is regarded as the department from hell. For about twenty years, I am told, Justice was that department, because – at the height of the Northern Troubles – it was dangerous, personally, to the minister, whose drivers were always armed and who were supported by a second car-load of Gardaí with shotguns. Plus, precedent-setting (and headline-creating) cases constantly surfaced in the courts. Nobody in their right mind, went the received wisdom at the time, would ever take Justice. This, despite the fact that Michael Noonan, Pádraig Flynn and Máire Geoghegan-Quinn had a grand time as ministers for Justice. On the other hand, John O'Donoghue and Nora Owen didn't. Mainly because each had to face the other across the floor of the house.

If I were offered a ministry, I'd always choose Justice. Because all you have to do is ring up the Commissioner and ask, 'How are the Guards today. Oh good. Tell them I was asking for them. I'll be at home.' You want to keep your head down. After all, what are you in charge of? The cops. And you can't interfere with them.

I lie, of course. As Minister for Justice you are in charge of prisons (which in my opinion are a complete waste of time – ask John Lonergan, the Governor of Mountjoy) of prison policy (whether or not you supply Methadone) and advising the government on the kind of wider policies that would prevent people becoming criminals.

Whereas in the past, the Department of Justice was the one to be avoided at all costs, now it's the Department of Health, or Angola, as Brian Cowen called it. As Minister for Health, you're knee-deep in trouble every day. No. You're actually neck-deep and you're standing on your head. Mícheál Martin survived it by being relentlessly pleasant to everybody, no matter what they said about him, and by creating six million taskforces to explore every problem. Mary Harney thought she had sorted everything when she created the Health Services Executive: from that point on, no Minister for Health could be held responsible for the problems of the individual patient in an individual hospital. Except that the law of unintended consequences, as always, kicked in, so that she's now responsible, not just for what happens in Accident and Emergency in the Mater on a bad weekend but for the fact that the HSE didn't solve whatever caused it.

Coming up to the 2007 general election the word was that Mary Harney would be erased and her party, the PDs, decimated because of health service problems. That didn't happen. Mary Harney went right back into the Department of Health and Children, having saved her seat. Many voters believed that if she couldn't get Health right, nobody could. Other Progressive Democrats, not directly associated with Health, lost their seats. But they lost their seats for reasons that were much more complex and interrelated than public rage over the health service. They lost because another candidate in their area got the wind beneath their wings – as did John Gormley against Michael McDowell. Or because another party ran a better local campaign. Or – above all – because they had become an uninteresting part of the establishment, and while the electorate opted, for the most part, to hang on to the Fianna Fáil bit of the establishment, they opted against retaining the Progressive Democrat element. But the bottom line is that the electorate returned Mary Harney to office, returned Fianna Fáil to office and returned the PDs – the few of them who were left – to office, whereas Liam Twomey, the Fine Gael guy who had spent the previous six months highlighting precisely the problems in the health service didn't get elected at all. Go figure.

That's the thing about the 2007 election that drives me absolutely scatty. If the Irish had done anything other than return Fianna Fáil and the PDs to office, the entire planet would have decided we were nuts. To be at a point where the country was as successful as it's ever been and take action against the government responsible would make no sense. To be at a point where the economy was clearly heading for tough times and to take a risk on parties which by the nature of FF dominance in recent years were inexperienced would have made no sense either.

However, the electorate did deliver a nuanced result. Fianna Fáil and the PDs lost, between them, several seats, while Fine Gael gained a large number of seats. The media coverage of the election results failed to reflect this accurately. Fianna Fáil did not win the election. But by *not* winning the election, they put themselves in a better position than if they had achieved an overall majority. They went back into office with Mary Harney and John Gormley bolted to their hip. (Plus Trevor Sargent in Food and Eamon Ryan as Minister for Communications, Energy and Natural Resources.) This ensures that the two ministries likely to be most problematic in the coming years are owned by non-Fianna Fáilers. Fianna Fáil is fantastic at collegial responsibility, while allowing blame to settle like an unseen smog around the heads of the ministers who don't belong in the Republican Party. John Gormley, from the moment he took over the Department of the Environment (arriving, admirably, on the bike it is suspected he takes to bed with him) was enmeshed in controversy because he had to push through the M3 roadway through the Hill of Tara, having spent the previous years opposing it. Within weeks of his appointment, satellite photographs established that the ice cap at the North Pole, which used to be one and a half million square miles, has shrunk in a couple of years to a million square miles. Climate change requires radical action. Like discouraging air travel. John Gormley is caught between a rock and a hard place and in that situation, Fianna Fáil will give him every help short of assistance.

The problem about going into coalition with Fianna Fáil is that the first, fine, careless rapture is mighty. The smaller party holds the whip hand, or believes it does. Its desired policy initiatives get fast-tracked. After the first fine careless rapture, it may take a while for the smaller party to wither and die, but it always suffers. The bell curve of the Progressive Democrats should serve as a warning to other small parties. But, of course, it won't. Because the excitement offered by the prospect of sitting around the Cabinet table creates its own blinkers. A few individuals become ministers and may – as was the case with the PDs – radically change national policy in areas like taxation and regulation.

I'm not suggesting, as others have, that Fianna Fáil is like a preying mantis, biting the head off its partner after sex. It's a wider issue. Ireland plays with small emerging parties the way a child plays with a new toy but tends to go back to its old favourites after a while. In 2008, thirty-year-old voters had no recollection of the rolling series of monster meetings that created excitement around the set-up of the PDs. They had no recollection of Des O'Malley's pulling of the plug on Charles Haughey's career. Nor of Mary Harney's refusal to go along with the Bertie Bowl. The PDs had lost their unique selling proposition, and died away to nothing while the nation watched. Without much interest.

6

The Myth of Leaflets,
Newsletters, Posters and Slogans

Once you've swallowed the myths and been chosen to stand for election, you get to the mechanics of actually being elected. That usually starts with making An Post happy. An Post loves elections. Particularly general elections. The amount of bumf they have to deliver to houses around the country multiplies to an incredibly profitable extent.

An Post, of course, does not care that most of that bumf ends up in the green wheelie bins outside the recipients' front doors. That's because, compared to the ESB bill or a statement from the stockbroker, a political leaflet is of minor interest to most householders.

Leaflets are grand at a local level for name recognition: 'Oh look, there's What's-his-Features on me doorstep.' It doesn't necessarily result in you making a conscious decision to vote for What's-his-Features but a basic principle of marketing is that the more familiar you are with a brand or a name, the more likely you are to commit to that brand or name.

Luck plays a major part in this. An Post cannot do more than throw the leaflets in through the letterbox. Chance dictates that What's-his-Feature's leaflet ends face up or face down. If the

Force is with a particular candidate, their leaflet lands face up and is lying on top of Who's-her-Face's, completely concealing the missive from some other political party animal.

Leaflets are the greatest demonstration of contagion in politics and it's a sector with more than its fair share of contagion. The first thing any political candidate does, when they plan a leaflet, is get hold of everybody else's leaflets, even if they have to dig out stuff from the last election. They then slavishly copy. Except that they don't copy just one leaflet. They copy *every* leaflet.

This results in a stereotype leaflet which leads with a carefully posed close-up of the candidate on the first fold. The candidate looks cleaner, prettier, sexier and more edible than they ever look in real life. If the candidate has run for election more than once, they also look a hell of a lot younger than they do in real life, because they keep using the photograph they really liked the first time around.

The leaflet heavily stresses, on that presenting surface, the logo of their political party. (This isn't always true. Time was when Fianna Fáil's reputation was so tarnished, the logo shrank to whatever size would remind the faithful while not irritating the hell out of the unfaithful.)

It also carries a slogan. Joe Bloggs, committed to Bugginsville. Joe Bloggs, active in Bugginsville. Joe Bloggs the future of Young Bugginsville. Bugginsville has to get mentioned to show commitment to the area, since all politics is local.

Inside, Joe Bloggs's autobiography is spread over one or more folds.

He is the son of Daragh and Muireann Bloggs, went to school, went to college, played football, headed the local group of farmers/Fianna Fáilers/Credit Union/stamp collectors.

If he has collected for a charity or undertaken a trek across the Bog of Allen for one, that gets mentioned, too. The only thing that doesn't get mentioned is any failure, setback or cock-up Bloggs may have ever had. He may have had ASBOS, his driver's licence may be covered in penalty points, he may be 'known to the Gardaí' and a number of former girlfriends would dish the dirt on him given half a chance but, as far as the leaflet is concerned, Joe's up there between Michael the Archangel and Pádraic Pearse, as far as flawlessness goes.

The leaflet is decorated with photographs of Joe in appropriate settings. Receiving the Cleanest Wheelie Bin Award. Or, if he's already a local councillor, *presenting* the Cleanest Wheelie Bin Award. Having his hand shaken by the party leader or some other worthy. Or posed in the centre of his family. Joe will never be portrayed, in his own leaflet, with a) a drink in his hand, b) at the wheel of his show-off car or c) doing something elitist like riding a horse.

Then comes the issues section of the leaflet, where Joe shows his knowledge of and concern about every pothole in every constituency boreen. He also demonstrates his support for the more popular policies promulgated by his party and studiously avoids mention of any policies that might get up the nose of any of his constituencies.

After that, depending on who Joe can press into service, come the validations from VIPs. Anybody Joe has ever met and been civil to provides a two-line quotation establishing that Joe is hard-working, committed, idealistic and visionary.

Last fold tells you how you can reach Joe at any hour of the day or night if the longing comes on you to share your problems with him.

Sounds familiar? Sorry, but that's the reality. The variations between leaflets usually come about because of Joe's age and experience. If he's young and hasn't done much, the pictures and the print are big. If he's been around a while, the leaflet is much more crowded with tiny print.

Creativity? Comedy? Forget it. Political leaflets don't waste their time trying to be interesting or engaging to the voter. They just exist. The candidate who takes a risk and sets out to be different has yet to be found.

It's a pity. Candidates forget one crucial factor about the voter. The voter gives a preference, not because of what they feel about the candidate but *because of what the candidate makes them feel about themselves.* Just as products like Budweiser, with their talking lizards, give the viewer a sense of being cool and smart for enjoying the elliptical script, candidates' leaflets should intrigue, reward and flatter the reader, so they feel cool and clever for taking the time to read them and may actually quote them to a third party.

One step up from the leaflet is the newsletter. Political newsletters have a proud and lengthy history. Most of our newspapers started their lives as little more than political pamphlets, produced by individuals or – in the case of the now-defunct *Irish Press* – a political party. A lot of regional papers developed that way in Ireland and Britain and a version of the same process happened in the United States.

In between the era when existing newsletters grew into full-on newspapers and the present day, there intervened a period where the political newsletter started all over again, in a humble, not to say positively sordid way. In the middle of the twentieth century, politicians started to issue Roneo'd newsletters to their constituents. This was a primeval form of photocopying which produced unreadably ugly reading material. As time went on, computer-printed and photocopied newsletters emerged and the process took a quantum leap forward with the arrival of desktop publishing.

Although newsletters look a lot better now than they did in the past, they still tend to be of most interest to politically-involved people who want to know which planning permissions have progressed and what's happening about zoning. Assuming that these people have no better source of information. This isn't true of the majority of people today. Now, if you want to know who's got planning permission or what the local council has decided, you can Google it and you'll know all the details inside two minutes.

A few – a very few – politicians have heard of Gay Byrne's theory about media, which is that everybody in that business is in entertainment. Even if they think they're in news, they're actually in entertainment. The politicians who have copped on to this make their newsletters as entertaining as possible. Some of them include competitions as a way of engaging more closely with their readership. They have a point. The more you can make any communication with voters interactive, the more engaged the voter becomes with you, and one of the areas in which politicians spend the most money is trying (usually unsuccessfully) to create that engagement is through postering.

Posters are a huge factor in a general election, although their utility to local candidates varies. The big spend by the big political parties tends to be devoted to owning the most popular and impactful locations, into which they place massive posters making general points and showcasing their leader (if their leader is not currently seen as a liability).

Posters are the classic exemplar of the old axiom that half of any advertising budget is wasted and if the advertiser knew which half wasn't working, they'd stop wasting the money. For a big party that's been in government for a while, posters are a challenge. If they stress new plans, the Irish reaction is, 'You've been there forever and it's only *now* you've noticed this?' If they stress their achievements so far, it's like a spouse arriving home and listing off how well they've delivered on their promises to love, honour and obey: irritating and pointless, with the added complication that the listener can always come up with one issue on which the promises were decidedly *not* delivered.

For smaller parties it's simpler. The PDs had a distinct series of constituencies that they competed in. They had a very specific voter whose values they played out in political terms. The PD voter was middle to senior management, top tax-band with disposable income, believed that government should run the way the private sector runs and didn't care that much about the hardly-ables.

Because PD voters were well educated, they liked inform-ational posters giving them bits of statistical data with which they could crush dinner-party opponents. In addition, they liked a bit of fun. In the 2002 election campaign, this was delivered mainly by Michael McDowell shinning up lamp-posts with cheeky cracks at Fianna Fáil: 'We'll keep 'em in line.' Once they were joined at the hip to Fianna Fáil and the early glow of tax cuts had faded, it was much more difficult to do opposition-within-government and the Progressive Democrats faded.

Fine Gael's poster problem, coming up to most elections, is that the party is too cool for school, too clever for its own good. That was the factor that led to the 'Celtic Snail' meltdown. Clever poster. *Very* clever poster. But it was too big a leap for the bulk of the voters. If you take voters who are fat and happy and decide to convince them in one poster that they're miles behind the rest of Europe and that Ireland is uncompetitive, you're going to get laughed out of it. You might be right but as a 2006 book by Paul Waldman directed at the Democrats in the United States pointed out in its title, *Being Right is not Enough*. (The subtitle is: *What Progressives Must Learn from Conservative Success.*)

In 2006, Fine Gael gave every indication that they had learned one hell of a lesson from the Celtic Snail experience. First of all, they moved earlier than any party into the poster business. They spent a small fortune – no, actually, a *large* fortune – on putting up posters everywhere. The posters visually introduced Enda Kenny in a way that was otherwise never going to be possible. Although Enda Kenny has been as long in the Dáil as has Bertie Ahern, to many voters he amounted to a newcomer when he took over the leadership of Fine Gael. Appearances in Leinster House were never going to offer him sufficient opportunity to become a household name and an instantly recognisable face. Hence the posters.

They showed him on his own. They showed him with endless permutations and combinations of Fine Gael candidates. They appeared on hoardings and on buses. Moving nearer the election, the party bought spaces in bus shelters within each constituency to run large portrait posters of individual candidates. With the exception of one poster, which took too intellectual and ironic a swipe at Fianna Fáil, Fine Gael's pre-election poster use was streets ahead of what they – or any other party – had achieved up to that point.

That success story is rare. Usually, the posters that are hugely memorable are the ones that are bad.

They become remembered because as soon as a poster goes up, media starts trying to dig spin-doctors up from the tombs in which many of them think we hide, drinking fresh blood from comely maidens. We are all then asked to drop the comely maiden and race to their studios to 'comment on the poster'. Because we need the appearance fee, we don't give them the obvious answer ('It's a bloody picture with a phrase over it and unless the party leader is naked or shooting heroin straight into his forehead, then it ain't going to make much difference.') Instead we trot out to the station and discuss the branding and slogans. A simple, clear understandable slogan is no use for discussion. 'A lot done, more to do' (Fianna Fáil's 2002 slogan) is the perfect example. It's simple and self-explanatory. On the other hand, Fine Gael's slogan for the same election was poor: 'Vision with purpose'. Because it was weak it allowed commentators to discuss the nature of its weakness. 'What does it mean?'; 'What purpose are they referring to?'; 'Have they got a purpose?;' If so, do they even know what it is?' – and so on. This rolling discussion makes the poster memorable. You might even argue that it thereby makes it more successful than a good poster. What was the Labour slogan for this election? Or the Green poster? Do *you* remember?

During the Lisbon Referendum campaign, the Libertas approach to postering knocked spots off all of the experienced political parties pushing for a 'Yes' vote. Before the campaign was even properly underway, they ran huge posters of Bertie Ahern and Enda Kenny, with captions suggesting that Lisbon was good for them but not good for you, the voter. They created fear and loathing from the start and continued that theme relentlessly. The more establishment parties, in dire contrast, produced posters which made no emotional connection with the voter. Those posters were wordy, boring and had a tedious 'Do the right thing' tone. If no communication other than posters had been involved, the Irish public would have voted 'No', based on postering alone.

I have a suspicion that in every political party there is a press guy or gal who dearly wants to have the kind of breakdown that Dudley Moore did in the movie *Crazy People*. He was an advertising copywriter who ran out of ideas, so he started to tell the truth. This led to a campaign for Volvo that said simply 'Volvo: Boxy. But Good'. The agency had him institutionalised after a campaign the slogan of which read: 'Jaguar – for men who want hand-jobs from women they don't even know.' The twist of the film is that the campaigns worked. It would be so much simpler if the main political parties would do the same thing:

- Fianna Fáil: 'We'll do whatever will keep you happiest.'
- Fine Gael: 'We're dull but we mean well.'
- Labour: 'We wish it was the 1970s.'
- Sinn Féin: 'We don't shoot people any more.'

Many parties shy away from attacking other parties in their posters, because some member of the party, at a meeting to discuss posters, will claim (wrongly) that the voters will be put off by negative campaigning. Voters *love* negative campaigning. The more negative, the better.

The proof of this was the creation of the 'Swift Boat Veterans for Truth' group which appeared during the 2004 US presidential election. For twenty-five years, most swift boat veterans had been pretty contented with the truth that John Kerry had won a Silver Star, a Bronze Star and three Purple Hearts for his bravery in Vietnam. When he decided to run for president a newly-created group started to question that bravery. The group released a book entitled *Unfit for Command*, criticising Kerry, and launched a number of TV advertisements attempting to undermine him. The advertisements were bad enough for Republican Senator

John McCain to say publicly, 'I condemn the advertisement. It is dishonest and dishonorable. I think it is very, very wrong.'

It was exactly the kind of campaigning that focus groups object to. Except it worked. John Kerry had to spend much of his election campaign defending a glorious war record, rather that focusing on the election. McCain himself was victim of similar nasty but effective negative campaigning during his 2008 primary campaign, when a 'push-poll' was run asking voters how they would react if they discovered that McCain had an illegitimate child (a veiled reference to the fact that McCain's adopted child is of a different race). Push-polling is a tactic where a question is asked to create an opinion rather than elicit an answer, such as posing the question: 'Would you continue to watch TV if you read research that said it gave you eye-cancer?'

The risk associated with negative campaigning is that it can create a backlash. The McCain (Republican) presidential campaign in 2008 undertook automated telephone advertisements that called voters and told them his Democratic rival, Barack Obama, was linked to the 'domestic terrorist' (or university professor, depending on how you look at it) Bill Ayers. The Obama campaign publicised the hell out of the advertisements, and this, combined with McCain's stated dislike of negative campaigning, managed to make the Republicans look nasty and duplicitous. It is remarkable that negative campaigning can seriously damage one decorated war hero when it works, and seriously damage another decorated war hero when it fails.

Irish politicians can't buy the same kind of media exposure as US politicians, thanks to Irish law (but watch the parties use You-Tube to circumvent that pesky legislation at the next election). Second, negative campaigning has to be done by a third party. If a politician publicly and repeatedly engages in nasty attacks against his opponent it will damage him. If an 'independent' group does the dirty work the politician is less likely to be damaged, even if he has put 'this message was approved by...' at the end of their advertisements.

Ireland had never seen this kind of third-party negative campaigning until the Lisbon referendum of summer 2008, when we got our own version of Swift Boat Veterans For Truth in the form of Libertas; unelected, unaffiliated, with funding from unknown sources and a capacity to go fast and hard for the negative, emotive and frightening. Just as the Swift Boat Veterans For Truth made a presidential election issue of a war hero's alleged lack of bravery, so Libertas made a referendum about bureaucratic reform into one about abortion and conscription.

They had the advantage of having a single-issue election (which is what a referendum is) rather than trying to elect candidates. If they had been electing candidates, their very effective postering would have had to follow different rules.

Individual candidate posters have to do four things:

- Attract attention
- Make the candidate look good
- Shout their name
- Link them to their party

That's it and that's all.

Those four don't necessarily require huge expenditure. They don't even require full-colour printing. The Labour Party – inarguably the best at making their candidates not just look good but *cool*, seem to spend their money on great photography which delivers the candidate and a mood or atmosphere at the same time. They often run black-and-white posters, which attract attention by virtue of their contrast with the full colour competitors all around them, with occasional touches of red together with evocative use of the Labour Party's red rose logo.

That said, local posters for individual candidates (as opposed to thematic posters attracting attention to the party or its leader) are not there to look pleasing. One political party in the past made all its posters into minor works of art. The candidate photographs were mid-shots. Instead of just head and neck, they were head and torso. In the party HQ, laid out on the big board table, they must have looked mighty.

It was only when they were affixed to lamp-posts that the problems surfaced. The mid-shots meant that the face of the candidate took up only about a quarter of the space on the usual party poster, so people driving by did not get an up-close-and-personal look at the individual who was pitching for their vote. The name was so spread out that, when wrapped around a lamp-post, only the middle of it was visible. The posters were a disaster.

Much the same applies to the posters run by the Green Party last time around, when they seemed to be attempting to get wind turbines and tomatoes elected, rather than candidates. Getting face recognition for a tomato doesn't have quite the same pay-off at the ballot box as does getting face recognition for a real live member of the Green Party.

One of the best uses of posters I've seen was when Royston Brady of Fianna Fáil ran for the European Parliament elections in 2004. Whoever dreamed up his posters had put themselves in the position of the drivers who would pass them on the long, straight seafront road on Dublin's northside which was part of the constituency. Accordingly, they designed a series of posters with a different proposition on each, so that the driver caught the first idea as they drove past the first poster and by the time they reached number four, had a full sentence, delivered by the sequence.

Royston's posters were a clever idea but not a new one. The idea was actually in its eighties when Royston ran for election. The notion of building slogans or phrases on roadside billboards came just after the arrival of the Ford Model T in the US. The advertising company representing Burma Shaving Foam realised that the American public was becoming a motoring public and was spending hours driving (slowly) along very boring, lonely stretches of road, so they developed a billboard campaign that was based on a building rhyme.

Ultimately the creating of interstate highways and faster cars made road signs ineffective as it's awfully hard to read a slogan at 75 miles per hour when it's all the way across a four-lane interstate. Luckily for Royston, Dublin's traffic rarely gets above 7.5 miles per hour so people had a long time to reflect on his posters. The end result was a campaign that was engaging, pleasing, talked about. And ineffective.

Royston lost. Badly. Which proves that even the best poster can't rescue a campaign when it goes as off the rails as his did.

It's one of the mistakes of branding. People believe if they have the right brand the rest of the process must be a doddle. I held that belief until I had a brief chat with a man who did one of the biggest PLC rebrands in Irish history. I asked him what the secret to a successful rebrand was.

> What you do is you pick a name that's not going to be offensive to anyone. Then you make the product define the brand. When I rebranded Company X into Company Y, I can remember that at the first

press conference, all the business journalists present were very bothered at not having a storyline behind the choice of the corporate name. They kept saying 'But what does Company Y *mean?*' I took great joy at the next year's press conference in going back to that initial dissatisfaction. 'For all those who asked me last year what does Company Y mean,' I said, 'I'm happy to tell you, Company Y means £7.80 a share!'

Political parties, except the newer ones like the Progressive Democrats, inherit their names. The issue they have to face is supporting that corporate title with a slogan. A party is successful in an election or a government. The policy or programme works. Then commentators and analysts and graduate students writing theses look at it and say, 'Ah, the reason it was successful was the fact that it was called X.'

This gets embedded in the public political consciousness and eventually takes on the status of Holy Writ. In fact, the opposite is the reality. Calling it X didn't offend anyone and then everything else got back-loaded into it.

The really good slogans are the ones that are inoffensive. No more. No less. People talk about the Fianna Fáil slogan, 'A Lot Done, More To Do' as being a thing of genius. It wasn't. It was just inoffensive. It didn't over-claim. It didn't over-promise. It conveyed a simple message: 'We've done stuff. Now, we have to do more stuff.' Even non-Fianna Fáilers couldn't do anything but snipe at that.

7

THE MYTH OF COSYING UP TO MEDIA

Politicians and political correspondents have a tendency to overestimate the influence and hold they have on the general public. They talk to each other in a constant loop. The politician says a thing to his press officer (often an ex-pol corr) who tells the political correspondents something, who then print it in the bit of the paper read only by other pol corrs and politicians, who read it and think, 'Score! We're in the paper.' The rest of us just ignore them.

The political pages of the papers are like Sky News and dentists; it's nice to know they're there in case something goes wrong but for the 364 days of the year when nothing is happening we'd rather just forget about them.

Political correspondents are terribly enticing for the politicians, though, because they provide direct access to newsprint and they mill around the plinth in Leinster house like journalistic Brent geese: they're seasonal, they travel in packs and they have limited time to digest so they constantly consume and defecate. The real function of the political correspondent is to be the first ripple in the concentric series that forms public opinion, the first bees that make the quorum on the new hive. They are the ones the other journalists talk to and listen to. They are the ones who brief the presenters of the news programmes and the drive-time shows. And they are the ones whose opinions matter more than their words.

This is one of the paradoxes of the relationship between the political correspondent and the press officer. The latter try to get their words printed by the former. But those words matter much less than the understanding and opinion of the journalist who repeats them. If you are trying to get a politician a better public image you need the political correspondents to think, 'Wow, that guy is a sharp cookie. He takes no prisoners and he's insightful as hell.' You don't want them thinking, 'He's a complete pillock. Lucky his press officer is so good.'

And that's unfortunately what tends to happen. Thanks to programmes like *The West Wing* and people like Karl Rove (George W. Bush's chief spin-doctor) it has become cool to be an adviser. There's a whiff about the role now that you are somehow part of an unelected brain trust, developing ingenious strategy behind the scenes. To further that image a lot of Irish press officers have taken to walking nowhere in particular so they can have 'pick-up' meetings, in which they talk too fast and use phrases like, 'It's only inside-the-beltway-chatter.' This is slightly disconcerting when you first join the meeting. You feel like a six-year-old in the back of your dad's car, not quite clear where you're going and too afraid to ask if you're there yet.

To add to the perception of them as participating in a brain trust, press officers will often take credit for everything to do with the candidate; the fact that he's awake, not drunk and wearing pants will all, allegedly, be the result of an intervention by the press officer. (In some cases this may be the reality. I know of one press officer who used to comb the party-leader's hair. I'm fairly certain she checked to make sure he was wearing pants. I know of another who wired an alarm to the head of a candidate to keep him awake at press conferences.)

Sometimes a press office will go even further and confide in a political correspondent: 'Here's the smart, visionary statement we'd like you to print. Off the record it took me four hours to make the politician I work with sit still long enough to run it past him and then I had to explain the English language to him. And wipe the soup off his tie.' The end result is a press officer who looks like a genius and a political correspondent who thinks the politician involved is a cretinous dribbling wretch. This is counter-productive as the political correspondent will then get drunk as two herrings and tell every journalist he knows how the politician involved doesn't wear pants around the office and has to drink soup from a toddler's sippy cup.

The first rule of being a good press officer is be anonymous. The second is take no credit. The third is take all blame. If you are the press officer to a politician who is seen to be weak, tell the political correspondent how he eviscerates you for giggles. If he's seen to be stupid, credit him for the brains he has. If he's indecisive, quote only his decisions, not the process behind them.

You need the political correspondents to act as influencers on your behalf because the media that matter to politicians are not political correspondents or even newspapers. 80 per cent of people get 80 per cent of their information from electronic media; TV, radio and the Web. That's where direct contact with the public happens and not on the political programmes. *Questions and Answers* is watched by the same people who populate its audience; vested interest political groupies who think politics matters. These are not (for the most part) floating voters. Similarly, if you have stayed up long enough to watch *Oireachtas Report* or *The Week in Politics* and you don't have a direct link to the political system then you need to get a hobby. Or a cat. The media that matter are the likes of *The Last Word, Drivetime, Today with PK, Morning Ireland.* Even better is a programme on which you don't expect to hear politicians; twenty minutes on *The Tubridy Show* is worth ten appearances on *Questions and Answers.* It puts the politician in front of an audience that is not politically motivated and is therefore less likely to have made its mind up and it allows the politician to operate outside the standard dance of death that politicians have to do with broadcasters.

The dance of death is a simple one. A story runs in the papers that says 'Referendum delayed.' Straight away an opposition spokesperson will come out and say, 'This is shocking and exposes our children to rickets.' The producers of the afternoon shows will see that this is going to run high in the news list (because nothing else is happening) so they ring the politician and ask him to be interviewed about how shocked he is. The politician is delighted. 250,000 people will hear him for seven minutes. He goes on air and the presenter (inevitably) asks him what the problem is. Cue a long stream of drivel about how this is typical of this government, shows a total lack of political will and indicates how separated they have become from the issues on the ground. The presenter hears a barrel-load of predictable political guff and begins to panic that his listeners will switch off. 'So what would you do if you were in government?' he asks.

This is where the trouble starts. The presenter knows the politician hasn't a bloody clue. He only heard about this at eight o'clock this morning: how the hell does he know how to fix it? The politician then defaults into a speech about accountability and public service and the presenter gets madder and madder that his guest has nothing concrete or new to add.

After the programme the presenter complains about politicians never answering a straight question and waffling. Rarely does he pause and realise that his programme put someone on air who they knew was unlikely to know anything or add anything, purely because he was going to provide 'opposition'. And the dance will happen the same way tomorrow and tomorrow and tomorrow. News broadcasters allow politicians on air to give out about things they don't really know much about and then criticise them for being non-specific.

But they'll still put them on air because they need someone with a credible title to fill the time and the politician will go on because he needs the exposure. It's one of the odd ways in which broadcasters and politicians are similar. In fact the jobs of politics and broadcasting are very alike. Both are predicated upon being able to get a broad and diverse group of people to pay attention to you and then getting a large chunk of them to like you.

There is a certain irony in the way many broadcasters pick apart poll results and criticise politicians for failing to be more are rated by JNLR (Joint National Listenership Research). This consists of a research company going around asking members of the public questions like, 'Who do you listen to between 6.00 and 6.30 in the evening?' The results are then collated and the papers write little pieces saying *Meltdown at Radio One!* Meanwhile, teams of actuaries are busy finding different ways to parse the figures so every station can say they're winning: 'Hey, Fred, it looks like our show has lost ten thousand listeners.'

'Yeah, but we've gained a thousand boys between twelve and fourteen.'

'Brilliant! The headline on our press release will read, "Number one in the Teenage Market".'

When all the shows in the country have finished claiming to be number one in the Kilkenny nun market or the 2 am seventy-plus Mullingar butcher market, the producers and presenters have to try to figure out why in real terms they didn't do so well. If you're in RTÉ you quote 'market shifts and demographic changes', then keep your head down. If you're in the private sector you say 'Please, please, please don't fire me, I'll get the numbers up or you can have my first child.' Then you have the nerve to go on air and ask Brian Cowen or Mary Harney how it is that they are failing to connect with the public and why Fianna Fáil/PDs are clearly in free-fall in the polls?

Most broadcasters have an overwhelming urge to tell politicians how to do their job better and most politicians believe that broadcasters have a clear political preference and are out to get them and their party. The latter notion assumes that news presenters have the time to foster a vendetta. Most of the current affairs broadcasters I know spend much of their time repeating in their heads, 'Please say something interesting, you boring twit. The woman from *AA Roadwatch* has disappeared and I've got to get three more minutes out of this nonsense.'

The most famous filleting in broadcasting history happened because of this. Jeremy Paxman asked Michael Howard (the former Tory Home Secretary) the same question twelve times. After the interview, commentators talked of the genius of Paxman and there's little doubt that the Conservative Party decided the interview was proof that Paxman hated them. In reality, Paxman had been told he had to fill time because his next guest was late and according to him, asking the same question until he got a straight answer was the best way to do it.

This interview also set the broadcast record for the longest interval between direct question and straight answer; Paxman had originally asked if Howard had 'threatened to overrule' a decision to sack a prison governor. He asked that question twelve times in 1997. Howard didn't answer. In 2004, seven years later, on the same programme, Paxman asked the same question yet again, this time getting a straight answer. 'As it happens,' Howard responded. 'I didn't. Are you satisfied now?'

Despite how similar their jobs are, politicians and broadcasters do a good line in conspiracies about one another. The conspiracy theory espoused by politicians is that most broadcasters have a specific agenda against them and are effectively apologists for another party, spending their evenings plotting ways to undermine whichever party the politician is from. The broadcasters' conspiracy theory is that politicians are constantly spinning the truth and seeking to pull some unspecified 'fast one' at every opportunity. And on it goes, members from each side regularly talking of the other side as being as dumb as a bag of hammers, then attributing to the same people a capacity to conspire at a level that would baffle the CIA.

The conspiracy theorising got a huge shot in the arm with the advent of the Internet and texting. The Internet gave us forums like politics.ie where political and media groupies can pick apart every decision and statement made by anyone linked to politics to show how it was all part of a grand – and sinister – plan.

Political Internet nerds tend to include spin-doctors in the 'dense but conspiratorial' category. 'Look,' they say. 'Did you hear yer man [insert name of spin-doctor] on that programme talking up [insert name of favoured politician here]? He's been paid by that party for years and a secret party member since 1985. He's just spinning on their behalf.'

At this point it is probably worth doing the riskiest thing a person can do: defining a spin-doctor.

8

What Is a Spin-Doctor?

Spin-doctors take many forms. The first kind is the party member spin-doctor. They're the ones who have been party members since they were twelve. Who get all misty-eyed when you say 'Michael Collins' or 'Éamon de Valera' or 'Jim Larkin' or 'Bobby Sands.' Or 'Rachel Carson' in the case of the Greens. They know in their bones that their party has the monopoly on the Way, the Truth and the Light. They know every nuance of policy since the Civil War. They have survived numerous leaders and regimes, have been there in government and out and if you cut them in half they have the party name running through them like a tattoo on their innards. They are the ones who get directorships or become Head of Government Information Services when the party is in power and move into PR companies when it isn't. They know that they really lead the party and that the current leader is only there because they let him and he has marginally better hair than they do.

Next is the fellow-traveller. Originally, they probably got involved because they worked with a candidate twenty years ago and that candidate did well, dragging their adviser with them up the ranks as they ascended. The fellow-traveller usually has their own business (often PR or public affairs) or is senior in such a company. In the old days (before European Union tendering laws) they were the ones who waited for the lads to get into power so they could get state contracts. They're usually very close to the party member spin-doctor and attend meetings at his or her behest. They are almost always wedded to party policy and believe that while the party may not have the monopoly, it has at least cornered the market on the Way, the Truth and the Light.

Then there's the thrusting young thing. They know in their soul that they can do it all a new, fresh way. They understand new media and modern Ireland in a way the decrepit codgers who are already there couldn't. They have noticeable suits and interesting hair. They end up with the party not because of any major policy loyalty but because it was the first political party to provide a vehicle for their obvious gifts. They annoy the hell out of politicians because inevitably they will turn up in front of a politician who was in Leinster House before they were born with a list of how that politician could do his or her job better. However, because they were brought in by fellow-traveller, a party member or a senior front-bench member, they have to be suffered until they either become a fellow-traveller or disappear to write the novel they've been putting off.

The thrusting young thing didn't know there was a Way a Truth or a Light but now that it's been pointed out to him he wants to call it Direction! Honesty! Vision! and make it part of a viral marketing campaign.

Then there's the gun for hire. These are rare in Ireland but common in the US. They hang around political street corners waiting for business. They have a few regular clients but will work for anyone as long as nothing too kinky is required. In the US there's enough passing trade to keep the gun for hire in business. In Ireland they do it because it's a bit of craic and they like the guys they work for. The other spin-doctors tend to react to this one like Richard Gere's lawyer in *Pretty Woman* reacted to his client bringing a streetwalker into the Beverly Wilshire. They are hugely suspicious, as the gun for hire purports not to care about the Way the Truth and the Light and just smiles wearily when handed the Direction! Honesty! Vision! PowerPoint. The gun for hire gets hired when shit hits the fan and dispensed with immediately thereafter. Billy Bob Thornton plays such a consultant in the movie *Primary Colours*. His character, Richard Jemmons, sums up the relationship with his client (presidential candidate Jack Stanton) as he's leaving the campaign by saying, 'That's what these guys do. They love you and then they stop loving you.'

This group of professionals is often supplemented by broadcasters who have done some fairly significant fence-crossing. (Politicians often want the advice, or at least the affection of broadcasters.) Buckets of journalists and broadcasters have dabbled in political advice-giving at home and overseas. Many of them do it quietly and discreetly, in the hope that it will never be traced back to them. Of course, most political parties leak like colanders, so the names of the presenters, political correspondents, journalists and columnists who have served as subtle advice-givers tend to be an open secret.

The problem with most advice given by broadcasters to politicians that it's based on programme needs, not political needs: their advice majors on how to make programmes more interesting, not on how to persuade voters of anything. Worse, some broadcasters equip politicians with a grab-bag of specious tricks that are utterly impractical and ineffective. I regularly deal with politicians who are labouring to put the advice a broadcaster gave them into practice:

- 'I was told every interview was about scoring goals.'
- 'I was told I should just prepare stuff to say and keep at it no matter what I'm asked.'
- 'I was told I should ask them to repeat questions to buy time.'
- 'I was told I should say, "I let you finish, now can you please let me finish."'

The politician may have a sense, from trying to put all this into practice, that it has made them look like a bit of a berk, but they figure that since a radio presenter gave them the advice, they must have not done it quite right.

Political 'experts' assume that all spin-doctors do the same thing: sit around concocting lies for their clients to say, then race to the nearest media outlet to tell the same lies as a form of public spinning.

This is true of a very few spin-doctors. Most of them have a moral core prevents them from lying, stealing or plagiarising. Some don't. And they tend to get caught, for the obvious reason that if you're under enough pressure and scrutiny to have to lie, then you are under enough scrutiny to have that lie found out. Spin-doctors who believe that a lie will buy their client a solution to a public problem are wrong. It will not buy a solution. It will buy *time*. And the punishment will be more severe down the line. Bill Clinton's 'I did not have sexual relations with that woman, Miss Lewinsky. I never told anybody to lie, not a single time; never. These allegations are false,' was the perfect example of this in action. So was the late Brian Lenihan's denial which ended with a recantation – the famous 'on mature recollection' piece to camera – during his campaign for the presidency in 1990.

The difficulty for most people is understanding what spin-doctors are for. If they aren't crafting clever lies or advocating for their clients with the media, what purpose can they serve? Which is like asking Claude 'Butch' Harmon (the man who trained Tiger Woods) how he can be of any use to Tiger if he isn't swinging the club?

The job of the good spin-doctor is first and foremost to ask one question of his politician clients, again and again and again: 'What are you trying to achieve?' When a politician says, 'I should go on that programme and tell your man he's a liar and always has been,' the good spin-doctor asks, 'What are you trying to achieve?' If the answer is, 'I want to vent my spleen and alienate every floating voter watching,' then the 'You're a liar' strategy is a good one. If the answer is, 'I want people to think I have things to offer if I get elected,' spleen-venting is counter-productive.

That's the most important service a spin-doctor can provide; clarity of focus on an objective. Without this kind of focus, people naturally default to random gut-feeling verbiage. Of course, when you say that, the cynics counter, 'Aha, you stop people being natural.' Nope, not at all.

Let's imagine your brother turns to you and says, 'My bank is asking for a guarantor on my mortgage application, I'm sick of them. I've been banking there for twenty years. I'm going down there tomorrow to tell them to shove my account up their arses.' You then ask him what he's seeking to achieve. 'A mortgage as soon as possible,' is the response.

'All right, Hubert. Can I suggest you keep that in mind, cool down, meet the bank manager, explain your frustration with total civility and ask him, in the light of your twenty years with the branch, to see what he can do.'

If your brother agrees, have you stopped him being natural?

No. You've stopped him inserting both his feet in his mouth and causing himself enormous problems. He'll still have the conversation his way but he'll be focused on what he's trying to achieve, not on the joy of insulting the guy with the cash.

The next thing the good spin-doctor provides is an extraction service. Most political advisers believe their job is one of insertion. They hand their politicians briefing packs an inch thick. They tell them what they should say in interviews, on the plinth, in the Dáil, in meetings. They begin every-second sentence with, 'Here's what you should say…' This is simultaneously patronising of the politician and utterly counterproductive. Most of the politicians I know are smart people. A lot of them are well read, educated, eloquent people. In Ireland, being eloquent, well read and educated can be an electoral liability. We have a tendency to respond to great eloquence with cynicism; 'Yer man thinks awful highly of himself. I knew his mother. It's far from "vicissitudes" he was reared.'

The result is a number of politicians who deliberately seek to look way more parochial and dim than they actually are. Their accents thicken, their vocabulary shrinks and they strike an 'I'm only a harmless nice fella' pose. The biggest exception to this was Dr Garret FitzGerald, who not only used an astonishing vocabulary and statistical lexicon to make a point but often used them to make several points, not necessarily related but nonetheless intertwined, at breakneck speed.

Too often, spin-doctors want to turn their clients into cut-rate Garrets, stuffing them with data to be reproduced. If the politician doesn't own and understand the data, this is one sure way to make them embarrass themselves in public. As soon as any supplementary question arises from something the politician says it takes them on to shaky ground as they cannot possibly have memorised enough 'lines' to fill an entire interview.

Cyrano de Bergerac got around this problem by hiding in a hedge to feed lines to Baron de Neuvillette. So far RTÉ have failed to provide in-studio hedges for political advisers. Until they do, inserting words into a politician is not going to work.

The spin-doctor should seek to *extract* from the politician the words, themes and attitude that will help them to achieve their objective. It's a bit like reading a joke from a magazine. The first time you tell it, it doesn't quite work. You have to get a 'feel' for it. You have to turn the printed words into your own. You have to get a handle on the timing, the punchline, the likely reaction. Once you've told it once or twice, you know the pattern of it and can do it easily from then on. So it is with interviews and appearances. The spin-doctor should be extracting the best from his client and then getting the client comfortable with what has been extracted.

The next task of the good spin-doctor is stripping away guff from around his client. Politicians attract guff. A myriad people, inside the party and out, believe they have the crucial addition to every speech, every interview, every press release. This turns the communications into a patchwork of well-meaning, dis-connected, impenetrable overkill.

US Presidential speechwriter Peggy Noonan, when she worked for Ronald Reagan, had to cope with a bevy of well-meaning political aides, all of whom thought they could add to Noonan's speeches, most notably on the day of the Challenger disaster, when the space shuttle blew up seconds after the launch. Noonan had to create a speech within minutes and, despite the time constraint, produced a work of art.

There's a coincidence today. On this day three hundred and ninety years ago, the great explorer Sir Francis Drake died aboard ship off the coast of Panama. In his lifetime the great frontiers were the oceans and a historian later said, 'He lived by the sea, died on it and was buried in it.' Well, today, we can say of the Challenger crew: Their dedication was, like Drake's, complete. The crew of the space shuttle Challenger honoured us by the manner in which they lived their lives. We will never forget them, nor the last time we saw them, this morning, as they prepared for their journey and waved goodbye and 'slipped the surly bonds of earth' to 'touch the face of God'.

Simple. Moving. Memorable. Except that an eager 'helper' tried to insert another phrase before 'touch the face of God'. He wanted to add 'to touch someone – to touch the face of God'. Why? Because he'd heard the phrase in a TV advertisement for AT&T.

This lethal eagerness to insert more and more leads to press release headlines like 'Infrastructural spend insufficient to meet community development objectives' and Ard-Fheis speeches with links like 'moving to the issue of economic exclusion zones and their impact on regional fisheries'. It has to be the spin-doctor who says, 'I don't give a rat's ass who thinks regional fisheries have a place in the leader's annual address. It doesn't fit with the theme of the speech, it is irrelevant to everyone outside Killybegs and I'll walk now if it goes in.' This may well fit with what the politician thinks but can't say because if he spikes it he will offend a party colleague. If the spin-doctor spikes it, the politician can blame him and end up with a better speech.

If the spin-doctor can do all that he's good. If he can think strategically he's brilliant. Strategy is a word regularly stretched beyond reason. Businesses have marketing strategies, communications strategies, advertising strategies, customer strategies, brand strategies. In reality these tend to be tactics. Not strategies. Good strategy is something rarely seen. A plan is not a strategy unless it's long-term, makes provision for its effect and how others will react to it and incorporates those predicted effects and reactions into the plan.

That's incredibly difficult to do. It requires a certain genetic luck few come equipped with. Some few politicians and spin-doctors can do strategy. I once watched a politician plot out how he would deal with a competitor for a front-bench position. He forecast the likely mistakes his rival would make, how his colleagues would react to those mistakes, how he could capitalise on that reaction and the effect this would have on all his colleagues. He then talked through which new supporter would talk to each of the colleagues who would resent him, which of them would then come to support him and which of them wouldn't. Eighteen months later it panned out exactly as he predicted and he got promoted.

If you want the perfect spin-doctor you get one who can do all the above. And then you hope they can write a video script, have a decent understanding of TV, Web and advertising production, can write great speeches, features and copy to a deadline, can develop relationships with people and motivate the people around them, understand public relations and know Irish politics and the Irish political system. If you find such a beast, keep it. Have it canonised. And hope it remains anonymous.

Consultants should follow the line in the movie *The Usual Suspects*, where someone says that the greatest trick the devil ever pulled was convincing the world that he didn't exist. That's the task of a good political consultant: to convince the world he or she doesn't exist; to stifle the egotistical desire to be seen as the power behind the throne, the transformer, the catalyst, the string-puller.

9

Why Ireland Is Different

In Ireland, political parties are allowed to spend enormous amounts of money on postering, which, as we've seen, has a limited pay-off, but are not allowed to spend any money on radio or TV advertisements. This makes no sense at all.

Radio is arguably the best attitude-and-behaviour change medium available. But the parties can't use it. (Except for a bizarre input at odd times on a couple of pre-election days taking the form of a party political broadcast.) Newspapers, on the other hand, tend to be employed to carry versions of the party posters rather than true newspaper advertisements.

These confusing constraints mean that a good part of the political message of any party or candidate has to be run through a filter known as a journalist. The good spin-doctor is the one who realises that the first task is to change the mindset not of the voter but of the political reporters. If the political reporters begins to think differently, this is reflected in their coverage, influences the rest of media – because journalists feed into and off each other – and ultimately informs the views of the voter.

It's almost like gaming a market and shares the tendency stock markets have of becoming victims of the self-fulfilling prophecy. If enough people who are seen to be senior investors fall out of a market, the market will follow that trend because it believes people in the know are doing it. In the same way, without even particularly noticing that they're doing it, Irish political reporters can game their own market.

It happened with Fine Gael after the last election. After the first year of recovery, features began to appear about Enda Kenny and about Fine Gael that said, 'They're not quite cutting it, they're not what they should be, the party's weak, it's vacillating. These features were written in the tone of, 'We were hoping for more. We wanted so much more, we hope they can get their act together.'

Of course, every time they wrote that, they fulfilled their own prophecy because readers would begin to say, 'Fine Gael are weak.' A feedback loop happened, with the reporters and the people all agreeing with each other. Once Fine Gael managed to break that, they started to get a (marginally) more receptive media.

A crystallised media attitude to a party or person can be the biggest advantage or disadvantage the party or person will ever get. There's an old cliché: 'If you get the reputation of being an early riser you can sleep till noon' that applies absolutely to the media view of politics. Once Bertie Ahern got the reputation of political genius, everything he did subsequently was interpreted as part of that genius. Likewise, once the world decided that Sarah Palin was a twit, everything she said thereafter was assumed to be stupid, whether or not that was actually the case.

Changing someone's view is extremely difficult because it is contingent on them having the ability to accept that their former view was wrong. I once heard of an international motivational trainer who ran courses for individuals and business people that cost €15,000 per week. It is my belief that a price-tag that high almost guarantees satisfaction, as anyone dissatisfied would have to come home to friends and family and admit that their judgement was so poor that they had thrown away fifteen grand on nothing. Very few people have the guts to do that. It's why Brian Cowen's initial poll ratings as leader of Fianna Fáil should have worried him and the party hugely, not made them happy.

Brian Cowen came to power with a reputation for straight-talking and bravery and a sky-high approval rating. That's a terrible position to have to start from. It is what happened to John McCain: his biggest pre-election advantage – that he was straight-talking – became a liability as he was faced more and more with the nuanced balancing act that is political leadership. And as he became more diplomatic and less specific, his former maverick status became a millstone around his neck.

By October 2008, Fianna Fáil's poll numbers were at an all-time low. That was not, primarily, Brian Cowen's fault. The national collapse into recession and subsequent swingeing (and wobbly) budget were the prime drivers for the fall in numbers. The problem for Cowen was that the one thing he had previously been known for dissolved in the crisis that followed; he lost control of the Fianna Fáil backbenches. A leader famous for requiring discipline and loyalty failed to maintain it and the public's positive view of him began to change.

Of course, party discipline is an oxymoron. There's a line in *Yes Minister* where a character, talking about funding for Africa, says, 'We need to be careful because the issue here is constant intertribal warfare.' The other civil servant asks, 'You mean in Africa?' and the first replies, 'No, in the Cabinet.'

Cabinets. Political parties. Until you work with them you don't realise how much their operations resemble intertribal warfare. Because they put forward, particularly nowadays, a brand that looks like a corporate entity, you assume a corporate structure. And it's only when you get in closer that you realise that there is nothing that binds these people together.

Maybe you have this loyalty in the US where there is a big ideological split – maybe it existed in other countries fifty years ago when you had the labour movement versus the conservative establishment. These might be ideological ties that bind. But in the Irish system – with the exception of Sinn Féin (and to almost every sentence you write in relation to Irish politics you could add 'with the exception of Sinn Féin') – internal discipline is somewhere between patchy and non-existent. Politicians may in theory stand shoulder to shoulder but in practice they'll eat one another's grannies.

Individuals accept discipline only if they see it as being absolutely for their own benefit. At the point where that stops you lose discipline and can no longer really control party members. With party officials there is an even bigger risk because they, whether paid or unpaid, secretly believe that they wouldn't lower themselves to be political candidates. They are the brains of the operation and the only reason the whole thing stays together.

There is a big risk that if a candidate is doing well (and this tends to be more floridly obvious in presidential or European elections) the party officials will run out and take credit and if a candidate is doing badly they will run to the media and explain that the candidate won't listen. They will also gravitate towards journalists who are personally engaged, which leads to an erosion of boundaries on both sides. From the point of view of the party worker, contact with such a journalist gives the snap and crackle of media attention and the thrill of feeding into a story, whereas in reality all party workers should be absolutely in the background and unseen.

It's the candidate who should have personal relationships with journalists. Supply relationships, not seduction relationships. The journalist doesn't have to live in the candidate's back pocket, just needs to develop a sense of, 'Wow, I know the real him,' sufficient to influence their writing and their thinking. This applies to smart candidates. On the other hand, if there is a candidate who appears to be smart, likeable, self effacing, insightful and is actually as thick as a post, they shouldn't be put in front of journalists because they will realise, 'Wow, dumb as a tree,' and start reporting on that fact.

In Ireland by the time you get to be leader of one of the parties who could be in power and therefore have the possibility of becoming Taoiseach, you've travelled a hard road to get there.

If you're Garret, if you're Haughey, if you're Lemass, if you're Ahern, if you're Kenny, if you're Bruton, you've had a long vetting process. You've had to get elected repeatedly in your local constituency; you've had to be a strong opposition politician on the front bench. You've had to have handled a junior ministry or a senior ministry and not screw it up and embarrass the government. You have to have the cop-on to see where the political infighting is going to happen in your own party and who to be loyal to, when to be loyal to them and how to be loyal to them. You get used to waiting for the knife in your own back. Once you've survived all that, now you can be Taoiseach. That means that anyone who looks at a senior party leader in Ireland and thinks, 'Ah, your man doesn't know what he's at,' is almost certainly wrong. You don't get there without guile at least. And for most of the party leaders, it's a lot more than just guile. In the US that isn't necessarily the case.

In the UK and to an extent in the US the parties are informed as to who they will pick as leader by the media and the public. They look to the media and public and ask, 'Who will be acceptable to these people as leader of our party and therefore get us elected?' The answer comes: David Cameron, for example.

When it comes to guile, the Irish political process matches *You're a Star*. The public chooses the acts that are going to go on to Eurovision. But in Ireland a lot of people in the general public call into RTÉ saying, 'For God's sake will you please take this choice away from the people, they don't know what they're at. Give it back to RTÉ because we used to win hand over fist when some apparatchiks picked the act.'

The same thing is true of how we pick our political leaders. So far we haven't chosen leaders of our political parties in Ireland because they play well to the public although this may be changing. The key considerations that get you to be a political leader in Ireland are the people you know inside the party, the relationships you have formed and the way you have handled the internal politics. These are much more important factors than how the candidate relates to the public.

It started in 1966 with a Presidential Election. Fine Gael's Tom O'Higgins stood against Éamon de Valera and startled the nation with a campaign drawing heavily on the Jack and Jackie Kennedy approach: all glamour, excitement and energy. Even the newspaper photographs looked different from anything seen before in an Irish election. It didn't work. De Valera won. But it *nearly* worked. O'Higgins came within ten thousand votes – or one per cent – of winning. And the word went out: the Americans know a thing or two about elections.

This campaign was largely driven by the phenomenal success of Theodore H. White's book, *The Making of the President 1960*. White's book was a first. A first to focus on the campaign strategies, statistics and dramatic turning points leading to JFK's election. White, a journalist and novelist in his forties, wrote a vivid and exciting insider's account which made sense of the outcome. It hit the top spot in the *New York Times* bestseller list within six weeks and eventually sold more than four million copies, transforming the way media looked at elections. Post-White, journalists concentrated on the back-room activities behind the front-of-house appearances. They went after the 'real action', probing for the advertising and marketing approaches, the gaffes and the contribution of media, to the point in the 2008 presidential election where the views coming from 'Spin Alley' (where the party hacks hang out backstage at the presidential debates) were reported on as fervently as the debates themselves.

Eight years after Theodore White, reporter Joe McGinnis went one giant step further, with his *Selling of the President*, describing Richard Nixon's 1968 campaign. Nixon's re-emergence from obscurity fascinated media and politicians alike, not least because he was coming from such a negative position: journalists loathed him and he loathed them right back. Nixon had learned one pivotal lesson from his defeat by JFK in 1960. In the big TV debate during the 1960 election, Nixon, his campaign exhaustion complicated by illness, turned up at the TV studio in a shirt that was too big for him because he had lost weight and with 'five o'clock shadow' because he had a heavy beard, whereas Kennedy, tanned and rested from a few days in Palm Beach, appeared easy, confident and handsome.

Although that debate didn't actually have the huge voter-impact later attributed to it, (Kennedy won the presidential election by only a tiny margin) Nixon decided that TV was the way to go.

If the print media could not be relied on to treat him

positively, he would major on TV appearances, which required no mediation to the public. He was described as depending on TV 'the way a polio victim relied on an iron lung'. That, in turn, required the services of media consultants. Nixon pulled in speechwriters and the creative directors of advertising agencies, whose job it was to confect a media-friendly image for him and make the best of on his (limited) sense of humour. McGinnis points out that 'Nixon could get through the campaign with a dozen or so carefully worded responses that would cover all the problems of America in 1968.'

McGinnis's book inescapably established the paramount role of the consultant as the person who could make the unelectable electable. While Nixon himself remarked, 'It's a shame a man has to use gimmicks like this to get elected,' the creators of those gimmicks moved centre-stage in American politics.

Political reporters hated it. And loved it. They resented the idea that they could be manipulated but were too fascinated by manipulation, when it happened, to shut up about it. Lesley Stahl, the CBS anchor at the time, was a classic example. She later wrote:

> During the 1984 campaign I decided to do a very long piece on President Reagan for the evening news. It ran almost five and a half minutes. It was a piece that was the toughest I had ever done on Reagan, maybe one of the toughest ever done on him up to that point.
>
> The thrust of it was that he wasn't telling the truth, that he was trying to create amnesia about his budget cuts and about policies that had become unpopular. We showed him in front of a nursing

home, where he was cutting a ribbon, and what he doesn't tell you is that he tried to cut the budget for nursing homes.

The next day, a senior White House official called to thank me. I said, 'Come on, it was a tough piece; what are you talking about?'

And he said, 'You guys haven't figured it out yet, have you? When you run great-looking pictures of Ronald Reagan, the public doesn't hear what you say. They just see the pictures. It was a five-and-one-half minute campaign ad.'

The notion that you could manipulate a nation by the use of clever consultants may have horrified Lesley Stahl but it also led to a rake of books about and by such consultants and to an ongoing fascination, on the part of Irish political parties, with those consultants.

We started loving the consultant-driven American political process back in JFK's time because it was then at the technological cutting edge. It has remained there ever since.

What distinguished the Obama campaigners, and was wonderingly noted by journalists, was that they didn't promote the consultants working for the candidate. They didn't leak, complain or claim to be the brains behind the man. That's unique in modern presidential elections, and in sharp contrast to Republican Bob Dole's 1996 presidential campaign, during which a disaffected speechwriter complained, in print, during the campaign, that the candidate didn't follow the speeches written for him.

The McCain-Palin campaigners were much less united and measurably less discreet. Within a couple of weeks of her selection as vice-presidential candidate, the McCain team were bitching about the Governor of Alaska, describing her as a diva who wouldn't take direction and didn't make relationships. The leaked disunity did the McCain effort no good at all.

Obama's campaign consultants were chosen one by one. They were chosen because of expertise, personality and affinity with the candidate. They were listened to by a clever man, who respected them.

But the essence of the Obama campaign was Obama, not any of the usual consultancy approaches, whereas the McCain campaign, much more consultant-driven, confused the public image of their man and – in its reliance on demonstrably un-truthful attack advertisements – diminished him. It's important for Irish consultants to know their place, while making available to their candidate the most up-to-date, evidence-supported methodologies.

American politics were the first to use TV properly, just as they had been the first – in the person of Franklin Delano Roosevelt and his broadcast 'fireside chats' – to use radio properly.

Roosevelt copped on, in the 1930s, that radio allowed a casual intimacy with listeners and he used it constantly. Sometimes, he even adapted speeches made during the week for his 'fireside chats,' including this one, originally made to the teamsters about attacks made on his pet dog, Fala. The broadcast made Fala into the most famous dog in the world.

> Republican leaders have not been content with attacks on me, or my wife, or on my sons. No, not content with that, they now include my little dog, Fala. Well, of course, I don't resent attacks and my family doesn't resent attacks but Fala does resent

them. You know, Fala is Scotch and being a Scottie, as soon as he learned that the Republican fiction writers in Congress and out had concocted a story that I had left him behind on the Aleutian Islands and had sent a destroyer back to find him – at a cost to the taxpayers of two or three, or eight or twenty million dollars – his Scotch soul was furious. He has not been the same dog since. I am accustomed to hearing malicious falsehoods about myself – such as that old, worm-eaten chestnut that I have represented myself as indispensable. But I think I have a right to resent, to object to libellous statements about my dog.

Churchill, around the same time, used radio brilliantly as a key element in his wartime communication with the British public.

But it was in John F. Kennedy's era (1960-3) that television became important and, in consequence, that media consultants, coaches and trainers became essential to presidential, gubernatorial and senate campaigns.

Oddly, among the plethora of political books to have emerged from consultants in America over the past few decades, few have been produced by media consultants. Most have been written by the campaign-manager types, each of them theorising about how certain approaches worked, why a particularly cunning plans was successful, or why it *wasn't* successful.

Campaign books sell because America has one of the largest markets for political writing. And there's always a massive new campaign to be managed. If you think about it, a campaign that runs in Texas is the same size as a presidential election campaign in France, even though it may effectively be a regional gubernatorial campaign. Every state election presents the opportunity for massive political campaigning, which in turn offers a strong market for political consultants and advertisers.

Partly because we have such an affinity with the US, Irish political parties assume that these consultants know a thing or two which might make all the difference to an Irish election campaign. They figure they may even know a *secret* thing or two. Irish political parties figure the flashiness of the American gurus makes them insightful.

And so, in every recent general election, one or more Irish political parties has, overtly or covertly, hired Yanks. The reality is that their flashiness may make them insightful into their own political process but has very little relevance to the Irish political process. Hiring them is a pointless mistake that we repeat over and over and over again.

The key insight it's assumed American consultants have is research. We assume they've got measures which will probe the demographic in such a brilliant way as to inform and change the course of the campaign.

This assumption is patronising to every working Irish politician. Ireland is, in fact, the biggest democratic focus group on the planet. There is a greater level of representation per person in Ireland than in almost any other democracy. We are knee deep in local counsellors, we are knee deep in local TDs. They show up on your doorstep. You might hate it but they do it.

Not only do they turn up on the doorstep, they listen. They listen because they have no choice. The Irish electorate is not behind the door in telling its politicians what it wants, what it doesn't want and what drives it nuts. An Irish politician doesn't need to tune into Joe Duffy to know what is exercising the mind of the voter at any given time. All they have to do is a quick canvass of their constituency and they'll get it in letters a foot high.

TDs and Senators have enough of a self-preservation instinct to keep in touch with their constituencies. They may not hit the doorsteps frequently (or at all) between elections but they run clinics, participate in local radio programmes where phoned-in comments keep them up to date, and pitch up at local functions to be buttonholed by activists. The end result is that each Irish political party constitutes one constant, rolling piece of market research.

The weird thing is that – in the run-up to an election – the parties disregard all that and pay out large sums of money to be taught to suck eggs by Americans who don't have anything like the level of insight possessed by any experienced Irish politician and whose research cannot ever provide the down-and-dirty information of a good constituency politician in this country.

The other profound deficit of American consultants is a complete absence of irony. Americans don't do irony. Like all generalisations, that one has its limitations but live with it for the moment while I give you an example from outside politics.

The story goes that when Gary Lineker came back, at the end of his career, from playing soccer in Japan, Walkers Crisps, a company which is owned by a US multinational, wanted to run an advertisement campaign with Gary Lineker being welcomed home with open arms by the entire populace.

A British advertisement agency, knowing the ticker-tape syndrome would not play in Britain or Ireland, came up with a commercial which showed the athlete sitting beside a little boy on a park bench. The little boy was eating Walkers Crisps. The advertisement first showed Lineker eating one of the child's crisps, then stealing the whole bag and running away with it.

This was pitched to the Americans, who were horrified by the concept.

'You can't do that,' they said. 'You can't have a sporting hero stealing potato chips from a little kid.'

The British advertisement agency assured them that the Brits would 'get' the advertisement. The Americans would not accept their assurances and made them shoot an alternative ending to the advertisement, showing Lineker handing the crisps back to the kid. Luckily the gutsy British director spiked it and the advertisement ran without it.

It's been one of the most successful crisps campaign in the history of the planet and it's always based on Gary Lineker stealing crisps, usually from small children. He steals crisps and runs away. He finds new and more creative ways to steal crisps from kids. That's the joke. Because Gary Lineker has such an innocent boyish image and is regarded as an affable guy, the contradiction works.

But the Americans still don't get it. They don't understand the irony and the send-up of the predictable that the UK and Ireland love.

Ireland takes that to an even more pronounced level than Britain. In Ireland, we live on a social discourse that is built largely on irony, wit and *double entendre.*

When you bring the big simple way to do things promulgated by American electoral consultants into that multi-layered cynicism, it doesn't work. The consultants will undoubtedly bring efficiencies regarding scheduling of events and issue-announcement but the big-picture stuff that works in the US does not work in Ireland.

If, for example, you have Air Force One arrive in Texas and

get George Bush to stride out into the sunshine at the top of the steps in distressed denim and wave, it makes the Texans go 'There's our President. There's our Leader.'

The same moment, in Ireland, would be unimaginable. If you were to fly a Lear jet into Killarney and have Brian Cowen walk out waving, the general reaction would be 'Who does he think he is? He's totally lost the run of himself.'

The artifice of the use of the plane would become the story, with journalists going to Patricia McKenna to get comments about the size of Cowen's carbon footprint and the disgraceful contribution to global warming. Nobody in America has ever commented about the speed of a motorcade but in Ireland, every time the cars carrying the Taoiseach or Ministers break the speed limit, that becomes a negative story.

Good communication, whether to individuals, groups or a nation, requires an acute understanding of the attitudes and beliefs and intellectual habits of that individual, group or nation. In that context – and because, at least in the beginning, we're terribly nice to American visitors – outsiders often fail to come to grips with the fact that the central reality in the Irish audience is its desire to tear down the successful.

It's the Irish underdog thing. We always want to tear down people we see as becoming too big for their boots. No, let's be honest. We always want to tear down people we see as *likely* to get too big for their boots.

Tony O'Reilly endeared himself to countless audiences by relating the comment made by a sports fan in the crowd at a rugby match O'Reilly starred in after he had become a wealthy international business figure. The man yelled encouragement to the other team to 'crease O'Reilly and while you're at it, crease his chauffeur, too.'

Ireland loves people who stay modest when they get successful. We love (or until recently loved) people like industrialist and insurance mogul Sean Quinn, who counters his possession of billions of Euros by talking about playing cards in the evening in a house that doesn't have an indoor toilet. We love people who seem surprised by their own success. We can't bear people who tell us how they made themselves successful. We can just about cope with books written by Irish entrepreneurs who stress the awful setbacks they experienced and survived but we'd really prefer if they told us how they fell on their backside. Self-deprecatory humour was invented to protect the successful against the hostility of the Irish.

If we don't want successful people to talk about their successes, we sure as hell don't want our politicians to behave as if they're taking themselves seriously. Advice about being Presidential and statesmanlike that plays so well in the US is a killer in Ireland. Charlie Haughey took himself very seriously, despite the *nouveau riche* ridiculousness of the way he lived, but he knew better than to take that behaviour into his local shopping centres when he was campaigning. In that context, he didn't take himself or anything else seriously. He bantered with the local oul wans and convinced them he was one of them.

It's only in recent years that this illusion was revealed for what it was. Charlie Haughey's legacy has been more and more tarnished as more and more of his lifestyle became understood. It's not that people have rejected all his policies. In some areas – particularly in his state patronage of the arts – his policy legacy stands up to posthumous scrutiny. The problem is that people stopped liking him because of what they found out about the way he lived and what that said about him. If he lived that high on the hog, they reason, he never regarded himself as one of us.

Bertie Ahern was a very different proposition. Central to his popularity – which was unparalleled in its longevity – was his apparent simplicity of lifestyle. Although media pundits bemoaned his malapropisms and consultants tried to make him more 'statesmanlike', he never changed that much. His fluency improved, down the years. But statesmanlike? Forget it.

Not being statesmanlike didn't do Bertie any harm. He was seen by the Irish public as unassuming. He got fashion things wrong. He showed up in photos wearing oul ratty wellies. He went for his pint down the local in Drumcondra.

Any of these things would be the kiss of death for an American president. They are the heart of what makes someone an Irish political leader. They are never what Irish political media define as the proper characteristics of a leader, because Irish political media has an ineradicable image of an ambassadorial and properly posh figure as the ideal leader: a Peter Barry or David Andrews type. The type political consultants want all aspiring politicians to emulate.

The source of this wistful conviction on the part of media and consultants that Ireland deserves 'statesmanlike' leaders is unclear. Sean Lemass may be the man who opened up the Irish economy in a visionary way but statesmanlike he wasn't. Jack Lynch may have been a marvellous hurler but as Taoiseach and Fianna Fáil leader, he was hesitantly anaemic, clutching his pipe like a lifeline. Garret FitzGerald couldn't find his own shoes or chair a cabinet meeting that didn't go on for years and require that a runner be sent out for chicken and chips. That Garret was the nearest we've had to a statesmanlike Taoiseach happened when the office wrapped itself around the man.

I would suggest that it was Garret's *un*statesmanlike idiosyncrasies which endeared him to the Irish public. I remember visiting his home, after he'd left politics, to interview him on camera. His office was a picture of confused paperwork.

The truly weird thing was that, hanging over all this statistical data was a mirrored disco ball. I couldn't resist asking him why it was there.

'For the parties,' he said, crossly, as if it was a given that a former Taoiseach would have parties requiring a disco ball.

Similarly, he was not statesmanlike the night of a big TV pre-election debate with Charles Haughey, when he had brought into the studio a killer document – and couldn't find it when he went looking for it.

Watching Dr FitzGerald groping through the pockets of his jacket may have infuriated CJ and somewhat discomfited the man himself but the viewers simply laughed and said 'typical Garret'. The disorganisation endeared him to them, just as the newspaper photograph of him wearing mismatched shoes made him more, rather than less, popular with the voters.

The Irish voter is more varied and perverse than the American voting public. Nor have we as predictable a political process as the US one.

For example, if you look at the 2000 American Presidential election, it is clear that Karl Rove knew that Bush needed to win a quarter of the vote over the entire US. There were a couple of states where the result was a foregone conclusion. There were a couple of states that had a floating vote. All the activity therefore could be focused on those states to achieve that small shift in voting pattern which would, according to Rove's calculations, return Bush to the White House.

In a system where you have binary opposition in the two parties – the Democrats being liberal, the Republicans conservative – and where effectively you have two big blocks of people who vote one way or the other, with smaller independent candidates like Ralph Nader doing little more than splitting the vote, usually the Democratic vote, what you have to manage is a massive but relatively simple political process.

As a result, the 2008 campaign, long before its end, was described as the longest campaign in US Presidential history, largely because there was no intervention of a candidate such as Nader to distract from its duration. The arrival of Sara Palin and Tina Fey's brilliant mimicry of her was, as a result, a welcome, if oddball, bit of excitement in the final month. The week before the election, the New Yorker ran a cartoon showing two voters talking: 'I'm a Democrat, but I voted Republican,' the cartoon figure is saying. 'I want Tina Fey to continue being Sara Palin.'

In other words, the entertainment value of *Saturday Night Live*'s take-off distracted from the relentlessness of the simple US electoral process.

In Ireland, on the other hand, we have a small but massively complex political process. We have tiny boreen constituencies – more than we need. Not so long ago, a group of Irish TDs and Senators went on a fact-finding trip to India. While they were there, one of the Indian parliamentarians asked them about the number of Irish elected representatives and was startled by the response.

'If we had the same level of individual representation that you have,' he observed, 'we would have a parliament of two and a half thousand people!'

We have a level of representation probably unmatched in any other democracy. More TDs. More Senators. More local councillors. More candidates. More constituencies.

Added to those phenomenal numbers – and the variety of contexts represented within this small nation – is the proportional representation system, which is the total opposite of the nice clarity of the system in other countries, where it's a case of X against Y and whoever is the first to reach the quota (or simply the person who polls the highest) gets elected.

Even then, you haven't completed the picture of the contrasts between the Irish version of democracy and the American version. In this country, we've had Fianna Fáil, Fine Gael, Labour, the Green Party, the Progressive Democrats and Sinn Féin. Six well-established parties with different levels of funding and different appeals to different swatches of the relatively small voting public. You have long-established Independents, who follow the pattern of neutrality adopted by Ireland during what we called the Emergency and what the rest of the world called the Second World War. We were neutral in favour of the Allies. Similarly, our Independents are neutral in favour of one or other of the bigger parties, some so clear in the bias of their 'neutrality' that they are often described as coming from 'the Fianna Fáil gene pool'.

And that's it? No. That's *not* it. We have one other complicating factor.

Single-issue candidates. They raise their heads in individual constituencies where, for example, the planned closure of a local hospital is a controversial issue and one or more individuals decides to run for election purely to oppose that closure. Increasingly, groups such as trade unions have at least begun to threaten that they will run single issue candidates in constituencies as a means of attracting attention to their bitter opposition to some aspect of government policy. In this situation, where the election of the candidate may be a long shot, the object is publicity. It may also have a 'spoiler' element, upsetting the predictability of the vote in that particular area.

Put any intelligent American consultant into that situation and the consultant will sensibly retreat to the safe, familiar areas like 'messaging'. Possibly the biggest legacy of the US system is messaging and the axiom that all candidates must 'stay on message'. This translates, in the bigger parties, to highly sophisticated use of mobile phones and e-mail to ensure that every local candidate for that party knows the big issue of the day as set by the party team and knows, also, that their duty is to stress that message throughout the day in their own constituency, to ensure that a) local media echo national media and deliver the multiplier effect and b) the unexpected distraction is prevented.

This has never worked here. It will never work. As far as Ireland is concerned, the messaging concept is nonsense.

At least in the US it's based on a little bit of thinking. The way the system works is that they look at the different swing states and they say, 'Right, for these guys what are going to be the crucial issues? What are the crucial statements that are going to swing them? What is their current attitude towards these issues and what do we want their attitude to be when we're finished this campaign?'

Once they define that, through quantitative and qualitative state-wide research, they know precisely where the campaign must bring the voters in those swing states. The next logical question is to ask what it is, therefore, that the voters need to hear to make them make that shift. The classic example of this process in action was the campaign against Senator Barry Goldwater in the presidential election of 1964.

What was necessary, to take Goldwater out of contention, was to make voters fearful of his conservative politics. So, where his supporters wore campaign badges reading, 'In your heart, you know he's right,' the opposing camp wore buttons reading,

'In your heart, you know he's nuts.' A television advertisement was broadcast showing a little girl taking the petals off a daisy while, in the background, an ominous voice did the kind of countdown the voters knew would precede the explosion of a nuclear bomb.

No matter what Goldwater did or said for the rest of the campaign, the voters had got the message and voted out of fear.

Advertising is just one of the channels which is virtually unlimited in America, while being tightly constrained in Ireland. In Ireland, political candidates cannot run radio or TV advertisements. They're entitled to run party political broadcasts but they can't do any of their 'messaging' the way producers of products can or the way American political candidates can. Which must mystify incoming American consultants nearly as much as it mystifies me. What does this ban protect the voter from?

In America, every local and national TV station can carry as much TV advertising as the candidate can afford and some of the candidates can afford an awful lot of advertising. They have fifty or sixty different outlets which can be lined up with the objective and used to carry the chosen (and tested) messages. TV advertising is used as the establisher, the scene-setter, the attention-grabber, with print and other media in an essentially support role. Ireland is so radically different that the messaging issue cannot be addressed with anything like the American strategic approach.

Another aspect of that approach that does not travel across the Atlantic is the bit that says, 'What do they think now and what do we want them to think across each one of our swing-vote states?' That's almost impossible to do here, because once you get down to the level of, 'Where does the swing vote live?' you cannot locate it in any one county. Ireland's attitudes, behaviours and beliefs simply don't cluster in that way. To a certain extent, they used to. In the past, the liberal vote tended to be in the cities, with the rural areas holding more traditional views. That is no longer the case so, these days, when you try to identify where the floating voter lives, you're into Noel Whelan's tallyman situation which is, 'Well, in Skibbereen, it lives in these three houses on that road and that small apartment block.'

Not only do you not have the big red or blue, conservative or liberal states in Ireland that you have in America; neither do you have the same sort of big chunky issues. The parties have moved so close together in Ireland that in the lead-up to the 2007 general election, ostensibly right-wing and ostensible left-wing parties competed to promise tax cuts and stamp-duty elimination.

The bottom line is that relying on American consultants to get an Irish political party into power is like bringing Ozzy Osbourne over to teach building apprentices how to lay blocks. It's interesting. It's newsworthy. It's expensive. It's highly entertaining. It's just not that relevant.

Because it's not that relevant, what parties in Ireland tend to do is lift individual elements of the American approach like messaging and try to make them fit the Irish situation, Procrustes-bed fashion.

Currently, the most popular element of what US consultants bring to the Irish parties is more and more focus grouping. Focus groups, as I will establish in the next chapter, are almost complete rubbish. At the end of the various focus groups, the consultant says, 'Awright, folks, we have looked at the various demographics and done this subtle piece of research. Based on that, here is the messaging that you need to deliver to these people.' The Irish guys go, 'Brilliant, here's a huge wodge of money,' and the US lads go off to some other country to help get someone else elected.

The difficulty they leave behind them is that, once you've formed your messaging for Fine Gael or Fianna Fáil or Sinn Féin or whatever party you're in, getting to the people is tricky. The US is well-supplied with conduits and they're so well-placed that it's as if the candidate could make a personal phone call to every voter.

In Ireland, our situation is so different, it's roughly the equivalent of having to use a drunken pigeon to carry the message. He might get there. He might not. He might get eaten on the way. He might get sucked into a jet engine. All the parties can do is lash him out there and see what happens, because we do not have such a direct conduit to the voter.

In Ireland, parties, particularly the poorer parties, have to use people as the conduit for the most part. People like canvassers. People appearing on radio and TV. People appearing in print media. The difficulty with print media in the first place is that Irish political consultants and politicians believe that they should be in the political pages. But the political pages are read almost exclusively by Irish political consultants and politicians. And they all preach at each other the messages that they've decided the other people should be listening to so you get into a fruitless feedback loop.

Even then, the difficulty facing political parties is how to get a cynical worn-out political journalist to say – verbatim – the thing the American consultant has defined as the message of the day. Typically, what actually happens is that someone from the back rooms of the party who didn't like the American in the first place and felt personally demeaned by the powers-that-might-be hiring him, goes to the journalist and says, 'Wait till I tell you what the American political consultant just told us to say.'

The journalist then files: 'Here's what the American political consultant told those half-wits to say.' The party then has to defend itself against the accusation of being half-wits dancing to an American tune and the messaging is thrown out by the side.

In the meantime, the local maverick (and each constituency has at least one of them) ignores the message-for-the-day and does something completely different, which proves to be a lot more interesting to media.

Sometimes, that something different is something vile, as happened during the 1990 Presidential election campaign, when leaflets were distributed which smeared Chernobyl activist and Labour Party candidate Adi Roche in a way which still provokes fury from the man in charge of that campaign, Fergus Finlay. The leaflets carried no name or address, so they were effectively an anonymous libel letter, comprehensively distributed.

It may not get that dirty in most elections but the campaign teams that meet in party HQ each morning invariably find themselves doing constituency fire-fighting, the trouble often caused by rivals from within their own party, rather than getting out the message for the day in the orderly fashion envisaged by the visiting American guru, God help his sense.

10

The Myth of the Focus Group

Bill Clinton famously described focus groups as 'a bunch of bull.' Joe Klein, the man who wrote the novel on which the John Travolta movie *Primary Colors* was based, goes further. He says that when you put campaign consultants together with focus groups, the consultants lose courage.

'They become specialists in caution,' was how he put it in *Time* magazine. 'Literal reactionaries – they react to the results of their polling and focus groups; they fear anything they haven't tested.'

Joe Klein said that focus groups make politicians risk-averse. No matter what they stood for or believed at the outset, once the focus group has spoken, the candidate feels safer talking only about topics, themes and attitudes which have 'tested well'.

The first issue that must always been examined when evaluating the contribution of the focus group to a campaign is the nature of the questions put to the group. What were they asked? What way were they asked it? The type of questions asked, the order in which they are asked and the manner used to ask them all influence the information that emerges from focus groups.

Coming up to the Irish general election of 2007, when any focus group was asked what were the key issues at that moment, the answers invariably included mention of crime. Why? Well, when you have members of drug gangs mowing each other down in the street and in their beds using Uzis, it does tend to bring crime to the forefront of the mind of the focus-group member.

In psychology, this is dubbed the *availability heuristic*. The availability heuristic makes us judge how significant an item is by how readily it comes to mind. Offered a questionnaire asking about the relative importance of issues, we will tend to give top billing to whatever the media prioritise at that time, simply because media coverage makes it pop into our heads.

If, however, the questioner went on to ask the same focus-group members, 'Are you frightened at home or walking to and from work or the pub?' they would have laughed at him. Which meant that crime was a talking-point about which people were constantly reminded but it was not, for most individuals, a voting issue. To cope with this, political pollsters have come up with a technique often referred to as 'temperature polling'. This takes the top issues and asks people to talk about how personally affected they are by each one.

So someone living in Foxrock may say their top issue is crime and their second issue is health. When you then take the 'temperature' of each issue, you realise they are worried about crime in a vague, national-policy kind of way and don't actually take a baseball bat to bed in case of intruders. When it comes to health, on the other hand, they are scared to death that if they break an ankle they'll end up of dying of old age or MRSA while they wait to be seen in A&E. The lesson to be learned from this particular temperature poll is that while the person from Foxrock may list crime as number one, the issue that will actually change their voting behaviour is health.

Drawing such a level of scientific inference from a process that is little more than having a chat with a bunch of people has to be taken with a pinch of salt. Particularly when those people are Irish. Freud allegedly said about the Irish: 'This is one race of people for whom psychoanalysis is of no use whatsoever.' Odd that pollsters will now rush in where the father of psychiatry reputedly feared to tread.

What matters, in campaign-planning terms, is not how frequently an issue appears in the media or how easily members of a focus group produce it in response to a general invitation to identify key issues but *how personally relevant it is to them*. If it's just a top-of-the-mind topic, what the focus group is doing is pub-talk overlaid with pseudo-science.

And, although focus group specialists talk about elaborate and subtle methods of probing into the real feelings behind that pub talk, what really makes someone cast their third preference in the privacy of the ballot box on the day of the election is unlikely to be something they're going to reveal in front of a bunch of strangers in a focus group.

In Ireland, we're talkative but secretive at the same time. We're not great at saying straight out what we actually think or feel. We are willing to talk generally but much less willing to cough up deeply held and perhaps embarrassing personal views – on anything.

Focus groups are a bit like juries. In theory, they represent everybody's peers. In practice, they don't. Just as busy professionals tend to get themselves out of jury service by claiming that their business or career would go down the tubes if they had to sit in the jury box for a week or longer, the people who can be persuaded to sit down in a hotel room, drink coffee and opine about the state of the world to a focus group facilitator are, by definition, less busy and more talkative than many of the citizens they're supposed to represent.

What the current reverence for focus groups tends to miss is the old Hawthorne effect. This was observed in work-study in the early part of the last century, in a manufacturing plant in a place called Hawthorne in the US. The study set out to find out whether workers performed better in bright light or dimmed light. Initially, the findings were encouraging. Productivity went up when the lights were brightened. But then it emerged that productivity went up when the lights were dimmed, too. Eventually, the researchers realised that the major influence on productivity wasn't the lights at all. It was the sense of being paid attention to that the presence of the researchers brought to the workers.

Observation changes the nature of what is observed. Being in a focus group changes what people say. Remember, a focus group is not a bunch of pals with a few drinks in them, talking privately in someone's front room. It's a bunch of sober strangers talking publicly in a hotel room. Wondering how the person next to them is reacting to what they're saying. Wanting to be impressive. Talking, yes, but also performing.

According to Joe Klein, one of the key reasons nobody should believe everything a focus group says is because its members are often 'reluctant to seem mean-spirited or prejudiced' in front of people they don't know. He says there is always a tendency for a focus group to become a civics class.

The tendency to become a civics class is best exemplified by the Bradley effect. This is the technical term to describe the tendency of US voters to camouflage latent racism when talking to market researchers. Or not. Depending on whether or not you believe in the Bradley effect and latent US racism. The effect is named after Tom Bradley, who ran for governor of California in 1982. Polls in advance of the election had him as the front-runner but he lost to a white candidate. The polling companies were then faced with a tricky question: 'How'd ye get that one wrong, lads?' They thought fast to avoid having to say 'dunno' and came up with the Bradley effect to show haw they'd been right but the voters had misled the pollsters because they didn't want to look like bigots.

In the 2008 US primary campaign we got another layer to the Bradley effect called the reverse-Bradley effect in which, apparently, black voters didn't tell pollsters they liked Obama as much as they actually did. Obama therefore did better in some primaries than predicted. Unless it's in the states in which he did worse than predicted. In which case the original (not reverse) Bradley effect purportedly applies. And if the pollsters can't figure out which effect applies they blame telephones. In the 2008 election, polling companies explained inaccuracies by saying they could only poll people with landlines so they had too small a representation of younger voters (who use mobiles). It's a nice throwback to 1948 when polling companies called the election in favour of Thomas Dewey. Dewey was caned in the actual vote by Harry Truman. Back then the polling companies said they got it wrong because only rich people had phones and that was who they called.

Remember that all this polling inaccuracy is in a two-horse race where the people are only being asked, 'Who'd you want; him or him?' It doesn't bode well for a more complex system, like say, parliamentary democracy, and it's been proven to go even more arseways in such a system. Just ask Neil Kinnock. He led Labour into the 1992 election with all the major polling companies declaring that Labour was ahead. Then Labour were crushed by the Conservatives. Once again the poll companies had to come up with a theory, fast. So they came up with: 'Shy Tory Factor' which basically says that voting Tory is the same in the UK as being a racist in the US: you'll do it in a voting booth, but you won't tell a researcher.

But at least the UK's parliamentary democracy is first-past-the-post. Imagine trying to poll accurately a proportionally representative parliamentary democracy? Surely that would be impossibly inaccurate? Apparently not.

Still at least all those polls are based on several hundreds (or thousands) of voters, allowing the weight of numbers to iron out inaccuracies.

I believe serious questions must always be asked about focus groups and about the person facilitating the group. Imagine: if you were to gather thirty people in a room and instead of chairing a discussion group, the head guy was to present each of them with a pill to take, some pills being placebos, some being a new wonder drug.

The reality is that if the head guy wrote up the results of that drug trial after a month, no scientific publication would accept it, because it wasn't 'double-blind', meaning that the guy handing out the pills knew which pill worked and which was a placebo. A double-blind trial requires that the guy who is handing out the pills should know absolutely nothing about which is which.

It's not physically possible to do a double-blind focus group, where the facilitator has neither knowledge nor personal prejudices. So things are going to be automatically skewed by the way in which the questions are asked.

We tend to underestimate the influence on our perception and – even more importantly, on our memory – of influential third parties. If you look at some of the major law suits related to child abuse and Satanism in the United States over the last ten or fifteen years, you will see that they frequently revolve around new concepts like 'recovered memory' whereby, through psychoanalysis and therapy, people have developed memories to suit the questions the analyst is asking which, they then believe, are real memories.

I would hold that a version of this happens in focus groups. Conscious or unconscious influence, either by a persuasive individual or by the group in consensus, *has* to inform the viewpoints expressed by some of the more malleable personalities in the group and – having expressed the opinion – that individual will thereafter believe it was a viewpoint they held before the focus group happened, even if it wasn't.

Because the idea of the focus group as applicable to politics emerged from the advertising industry, where it was used to test slogans and packaging, it's assumed that focus groups are an infallible testing-ground for leadership themes. Not so.

The focus group will always produce vanilla ice cream – that's what focus groups do. Focus groups drag their own members down to the lowest common denominator. That's true even if you're testing the marketability of a new product. Gather a number of people around and put to them a completely new concept and see what happens.

'D'you know what ice cream flavour we're considering?' you might say. 'We're thinking about taking raw cookie dough and shoving it into an ordinary vanilla ice cream – what would you think about that?"

The focus group is inevitably going to wince at the thought of what it would taste like. Similarly, were you to gather together a focus group and say, 'Guys, I'm going to make bacon and egg ice cream,' the focus group will tell you it's not going to work.

Ben & Jerry's became one of the bestselling brands in the world because they had mad untutored faith in products like Chocolate Chip Cookie Dough Ice Cream.

In similar vein, Heston Blumenthal, who runs The Fat Duck, the Michelin-starred best restaurant on the planet, specialises in bacon and egg ice cream. They can't keep up with the demand for it, yet a focus group would have prevented either of those products from being developed past the bright idea stage.

Focus groups tell you what offends them. They can't tell you about political leadership. All the great moments of political leadership would have been prevented if submitted to a focus group in advance. Take, for example, Churchill's speech where he promised the British public nothing but 'blood, toil, tears and sweat'. Focus groups are notoriously averse to negativity and promising people injury, effort, perspiration and grief does come under the heading 'negativity'. Yet, in wartime, that speech served to pull the British public into a commitment which was, as Churchill predicted it would be, their finest hour.

In the same way, then Taoiseach Charles Haughey got great credit – at the time – for going on RTÉ television in 1980 and announcing to the nation that our collective finances were in rag order and that it was now time to tighten our belts. People responded to that. They may not have responded with quite the same enthusiasm as Londoners did in the Blitz but there was a genuine willingness to accommodate what was, on the face of it, seriously negative, and take on the responsibility Haughey laid on them. Later, of course, when it emerged that, at the time he was wishing poverty on the rest of us, he himself was buying Charvet shirts and the best of champagne with monies donated by rich people, the glow went off the self-sacrifice he had called for. But we should not forget that he evoked it in a way any focus group would have rejected, just as they would have rejected the line in President John Kennedy's 1962 speech about going to the moon, where he said that this aspiration, along with others, would be tackled, 'not because they are easy, but because they are *hard*'.

Focus groups always give you blancmange. They cannot cope with leadership, genius, insight. The best example of it is always the corporate example. Companies that come up with new ideas and new products never do it out of focus groups. Ryanair didn't become the low-fares airline because they gathered together a hundred Aer Lingus consumers and asked them what they didn't like about the standard airline offering. If they had, the focus group would have produced comments about Aer Lingus's poxy uniforms or the music on the airline's earphone system.

What Ryanair did was come up with a single proposition and put Michael O'Leary in charge of driving that proposition bald-headed. The fares came down. The passengers whinged that they didn't get the same level of civility they'd have got on normal airlines. Indeed, they whinged that they didn't get *any* level of civility. But they kept flying Ryanair and in the process forced many of the traditional carriers to convert themselves into low-fares airlines.

Cast your mind back to the mid-1980s and imagine being in a focus group listening to the pitch for what would become some of Ireland's greatest business successes: we're going to make you pay for snacks; pay to put baggage in the hold; not allow you to book a seat; and make it a free-for-all at the gate. We'll also become synonymous with couldn't-care-less treatment of customers. Would you be the one in the focus group who'd say, 'Brilliant! Go for it!'?

Ballygowan's might have been: we're going to take stuff that comes out of your tap for free, stick it in a bottle and charge you big money for it. Back then, would you have offered to pay for something you got for nothing?

Esat's pitch would have been; we're going to sell phones (that at the time looked like grey building-bricks) to people for several hundred quid, even though they already have a phone at home, which is way cheaper to use. And we're betting that everyone in the house will buy one, even though they all have access to the cheaper home phone.

Everything new, different and creative gets shot down by focus groups. The steam engine, electric light, mobile phones, PCs, bottled water were all surrounded by packs of *ad-hoc* focus groups roaring, 'It'll never work.' It took Frank Whittle nearly a decade to get his jet engine accepted because so many people told him it was a pointless endeavour, destined to fail. This was an invention that changed the world as much as any in history.

Or take another example: Columbus. He pitched his expedition to the Spanish royal family, at a time when that royal family wanted more territory and – just as importantly – wanted to find new routes for transporting precious spices from the East Indies. They knew what they wanted, and what Columbus proposed looked as if it would contribute to them meeting their objectives. If he had been forced to pitch to a focus group, his chances of discovering America would have disappeared instantly. Because a focus group has no objective apart from delivering opinions And if you have no port to go to, you're likely to have big doubts about taking to the seas.

Focus groups can only reflect the *status quo*. What they're used to. What's safe to approve of. Which is why they can't manage leadership. Because leadership is sometimes about giving people what they *don't* want and making them like it.

Innovative product-development is the same. Marketing an innovative product is about knowing you have something great and working out how to sell it. It requires someone who has a sense of vision, ideas, ideology. Al Gore is the perfect case in point. He has become an international phenomenon with what is essentially a PowerPoint presentation (*An Inconvenient Truth*) that has played in cinemas all over the world and more speaking engagements at $70,000 a throw than he can find days in the year to fulfil. That's remarkable, especially when he's delivering the most negative of messages: if we don't get our environmental act together within fifteen years, millions of people will starve, drown or be displaced.

But there is no way he would have been allowed to do that while he was running for the presidency, because the focus groups would have registered negative reactions to his thesis and language. Instead, they blandified him to the point where he lost by 500 votes in 2000 and the news story became the hanging chads that contributed to his loss.

If Ralph Nader had not chosen to do his appalling ego-run and if Al Gore had been allowed to behave the way he wanted behave, given that 52 per cent of the US voted *against* Bush, Gore would have won by a landslide. Instead, he not only lost but left a memory of stodgy boredom punctuated by teeth-grindingly awful incidents like his speeches about his son's accident and his sister's death, not to mention his gruesome marathon kiss with his wife.

The stodgy boredom was undoubtedly caused by focus group research that squelched Gore's passion for the environment. The creepy self-revelation was undoubtedly the result of intervention by some consultant eager to humanise the candidate.

If he hadn't been already dehumanised by focus groups, the

crazy 'corrective' measures would never have been needed, the US would be environmentally better off and would not now be at war with Iraq.

TEN REASONS FOCUS GROUPS ARE A BUNCH OF BULL
1. A talking point is not the same as a personal issue on which individuals will cast their vote.
2. Focus groups tell you what offends them. Nobody ever created a great politician by obediently amputating their most offensive points.
3. Focus group research is tainted by the preferences of the facilitator.
4. Focus groups contribute to the myth of presidential leadership, adding to the belief that a party will win or lose an election on the basis of the appearance, wardrobe and rhetoric of the top bod.
5. Focus groups are necessarily *national* in their focus. But all politics – especially the third preference cast in any Irish constituency – is *local*.
6. Focus groups reduce individuality, turning all politicians into over-cautious, vanilla-flavoured nobodies.
7. Focus groups are anti-political. They discourage politicians from believing in and acting on the things that got them into politics in the first place. Imagine if Islam ran a focus group to see what Muslims should believe in? It wouldn't happen. We demand that politicians be passionate about issues – and then set up focus groups to tell them what it's safe to be passionate about. Contradiction in terms.
8. Focus groups are beloved of the suits within any political party because they reveal weaknesses in individual politicians. So Minister X gets known as 'the guy the focus group didn't

want to have a pint with' and the suits get to keep him or her off the box during the election.

9. Focus groups are not accountable. They are never retrospectively interrogated, as in 'How useful were those focus groups in preventing the meltdown of our politician party at the general/local/European elections?'

10. Focus groups, most dangerously, devalue the genuine research good local politicians can provide. Door-to-door canvassing, as any good operator will tell you, will reveal fast and furiously the real concerns of voters and their reactions to candidates, parties and policies. Except that most political parties don't bother putting a system in place to capture and organise this worthwhile and free information, preferring to spend money on the pseudo-scientific capture of collective pub-talk.

11

Clothes Maketh the Candidate?

We may – and some of us do – kid ourselves that we make our clothing choices out of our own individual tastes, uninfluenced by other considerations. But we're wrong. From the earliest times, dress has been used to delineate social contrasts. Dwellers in some medieval cities were subject to what was called sumptuary legislation. Those laws allowed only the gentle classes to wear silk or satin. Fashion and colour established age, occupation and rank.

The early blue dies were what the French call *pisseux*. Which is a pretty vivid way of indicating that the colour tended to run. Not that it mattered, since only workers in rough working clothes ever wore blue, which is why, to this day, we talk about 'blue collar' occupations.

Around 1400 AD, a plant related to cabbage called woad came into the hands of dyers, who grew it, fermented it, ground it to powder and used it to make blue clothing that would not fade or run. Suddenly, blue was no longer for the peasants alone. The French kings chose a powerful saturated blue as background to the *fleur-de-lys* and blue moved up the social scale. (Indigo later took over from woad.)

But it wasn't just colour that separated nobility from the rest. During the Middle Ages fools, jugglers, executioners and prostitutes wore broad stripes, whereas the bourgeoisie opted for plain colours brightened up with cloth woven with borders or all-over patterns.

Stripes survived in military emblems, decorating otherwise sombre, solid-colour uniforms. They also survived in convict dress. The stripes prisoners were forced to wear meant that if they escaped, they were easily spotted. In addition, the striped garb carried a daily humiliation for its wearer.

Throughout the ages, the church had an elaborate system of uniforms to demand proper respect from the laity. More recently airlines clad their pilots and co-pilots in uniforms reminiscent of military attire, partly to reassure passengers that officers were in charge of the flight.

Wars create their own fashions and symbols. The Crimean War gave us balaclavas, cardigans and raglan sleeves, the Vietnam War made imitation dog-tags briefly fashionable and the Gulf wars made camouflage fabric trendy for casual wear.

Now, politics has got in on the act. The legacy of the vanilla-isation of politics has been the creation of the political uniform.

People who theorise about clothing maintain that you can communicate a different view of the candidate by putting different clothes on them. It breaks down into a couple of broad headings.

The male candidate wears basically a deep-blue suit for more or less everything. It is the guaranteed winner, this deep-blue suit. But what you put with the deep-blue suit defines the way you want to be seen by people. If you go with the white shirt and red tie, you are the powerful leader. If you go with the red shirt and the blue tie you are the leader who is compassionate. If you go with the blue shirt and the blue tie it means you're friendly. And Tony Blair added the wrinkle that if you go without the tie and roll up your sleeves, it means you're one of the people.

There can be no doubt that these are the four states of uniform for a political candidate, if you're minded to wear a uniform. Some Irish politicians have deliberately avoided that uniform. Tony Gregory has always chosen man-of-the-people clothing, refusing to wear a tie in Leinster House, even when the rules required him to. Gerry Adams formerly specialised in tweed jackets. Members of the Labour and Green Parties are less likely than Fine Gael or Fianna Fáil to wear Armani suits, opting instead for more casual sports jackets and trousers, at least until they become ministers – useful also for cycling to work, in the case of the Greens.

In the United States, presidents have tended to throw in a workmanlike look, now and again, just for variety. So George Bush clears scrub at his ranch in photo opportunities, wearing faded denim shirts, blue jeans and cowboy boots. Bill Clinton was (unfortunately) photographed wearing shorts while jogging. Ronald Reagan was photographed in suede jacket and riding boots on his horse. All these variations send the message: 'I'm a man of the people, I drive pick-up trucks just like you do.'

Some of the attempts to look ordinary have backfired. John Kerry windboarding (something like windsurfing on snow) may have seemed like a good idea but in fact underlined the public perception of him as elitist.

Increasingly, in Ireland, uniformity is the order of the day. There's nothing more dispiriting than dealing with a group of Dáil candidates on a media skills course and finding that, while they nod their heads at advice telling them to be interesting, understandable and memorable, what makes them take up their pens and make notes is when you indicate that you're going to talk briefly about what they might wear on TV.

Most of what passes for sophisticated and focus-group-tested wardrobe advice for politicians amounts to the square root of nothing. My own advice to politicians is simple: don't wear anything that's louder than you are.

It is, of course, possible to wear something louder than you are by accident. On one occasion, a number of journalists telephoned my company to seek a comment on what the Head of the HSE had worn at a press conference. One item of his clothing was assumed to have some deep significance. The journalists were speculating that Professor Drumm's tie might have been chosen in order to send a message of disrespect to the Minister for Health.

What on earth, we asked, was *on* his tie? Looney Toons. *Looney Toons?* Yes, the cartoon figures. Aaah, we said. Aaah. Sorry, lads, Professor Drumm is not giving the finger to the Minister at all. Professor Drumm is a paediatrician. Paediatricians nearly always wear ties with Winnie the Pooh or some other readily-identifiable cartoon figure on them, so that the children they're examining won't get frightened. Sorry to squelch a good story but that's the way it is...

The problem is that a bunch of ungrounded theories led to clothing dogmas that have reduced the individual choice of candidates, generated healthy make-over businesses and created a weird ripple effect where other people decide someone got elected or failed to get elected because of the colour of his tie. This in turn feeds into the fallacy of strategy: some clever person caused this. The reality often is that the supposedly significant clothing choice was in fact pure luck.

The best debunking of the clothing myth was when Bill Clinton and Tony Blair were going to the same reception and they had been left out clothes to wear. It's a story Tony Blair himself tells. Blair said that he looked at the selection of ties and shirts and they were so Godawful he thought, 'I cannot be seen in these,' and wore his own stuff. When he came downstairs Clinton was wearing the worst of the ties and shirts that Blair had just rejected.

Blair asked him how come he'd gone with the awful clothing laid out for him. And Clinton put his arm around him and he said, 'Because, when this goes on TV at home, people are going to say, "Ah look at him, he has to wear what the local guys put on him, isn't he very kind."'

Now, if the president of the US is willing to wear what the locals put on him so the people at home think he's nice, he knows you don't have to wear particular clothing combinations in order to be seen to be powerful. On the other hand, there can be no doubt that television has changed the way we judge politicians. Before television, the public rarely saw their politicians in anything but black-and-white photographs and so tended to judge them on what they said or wrote.

Barbara Kingsolver, the novelist and essayist, has made the suggestion that television may have actually harmed the political process. She wonders why certain things are televised at all:

> If our aim is to elect candidates on the basis of their stature, clothing and facial expressiveness, then fine, we should look at them. But if our intention is to evaluate their ideas, we should probably just listen and not look. Give us one good gander and we'll end up electing cheerleaders instead of careful thinkers. In a modern election, Franklin D. Roosevelt in his wheelchair wouldn't have a prayer, not to mention the homely but honest Abe Lincoln.

In fact, homely but honest Abe Lincoln came under pressure from an unexpected source to tidy up his appearance during his run for the American presidency. An eleven-year-old named Grace Bedell wrote to him, suggesting that he grow a beard, since 'all the ladies like whiskers and your face is so thin'.

The candidate took the time to write back to her, thanking her for her advice, which, not having a daughter of his own, he wouldn't otherwise have received. 'As to the whiskers, having never worn any, do you not think people would call it a piece of silly affectation if I were to begin it now?' he asked her.

A good question. A question modern politicians should ask themselves before yielding to advice on changing their looks. It's not clear whether Grace wrote back to Lincoln but, one way or the other, he took her advice and grew himself a beard.

It does help a male politician not to be bald or ugly. Anyone who is going to appear physically in front of people benefits from being good-looking although it's not the be all and end all. This is not fair. But it's a reality. Pretty people are nice to look at. It's a fact. Therefore pretty people will get more exposure in pictures.

The taller a man is, the better. A study in the US showed that men do better in salary terms the taller they are. On average, men will earn a thousand dollars more for every additional inch in height that they have. So someone who is 6 foot 2 inches is likely to earn two grand more a year than someone who is 6 foot. (Obviously there are exceptions to this rule.)

It's also a fact that lack of good looks hasn't held back some great politicians. Look at Winston Churchill – a chain-smoking, depressive, alcoholic little fat guy. He got to the top by sheer ability and being in the right place at the right time – hurray for him.

John F. Kennedy had a rule every politician should abide by. Nothing was ever to be put on his head. Just about the only exception, for today's politician, is the hard hat on a building site. Hard hats look pretty good on most men and do send the message that you abide by health and safety rules in an area of potential hazard. However, if you're in the clean room of a computer plant, don't wear one of those HazMat suits that make everybody look like sperm and don't let anybody put a plastic mob cap on you. Your career is unlikely to survive it.

The other killer photograph, in Ireland, is the one taken when the politician gives blood. In theory, it demonstrates bravery and public concern. In reality, it shows the politician lying down (soles of shoes never look good) looking helpless and fat, with a tube stuck into them.

Male politicians have a far easier time than female politicians. At least male politicians have a simpler uniform. You buy a couple of decent suits, a few good shirts and bright ties, match them with well-made shoes, take care of them and that's basically it.

Pity the women politicians. Studies of how audiences view women as opposed to the way they view men, both on TV and in real encounters, indicate that most audience gaze patterns very quickly start to concentrate on the head and shoulders when they're looking at men. When they're looking at women, by contrast, they tend to continue to look up and down from the top of the woman's head to the base of her shoes.

I remember on one occasion sending a consultant from our company to meet a client and speaking to the client afterwards. The client mentioned that consultant, a woman, appeared to be very wealthy.

'Why?' I asked, startled.

The client was able to tell me the brand name of every single item of the woman's clothing, from shoes to handbag, from jacket to skirt, assuring me that when it came to her stud earrings they were definitely diamonds and that her bangles were three shades of gold. Not to mention the price of her Mont Blanc pen. Now, admittedly the client was a woman. This level of detailed (and costed) observation doesn't tend to happen with men. Nor do men have the same attention paid to their appearance.

It is much more difficult, particularly in the US, to achieve high political office if you are an unattractive woman than it is for an unattractive man. Cruel public comments are made about a female candidate's appearance, particularly if she is overweight, as is sometimes the case in Ireland, not least because of the long hours politicians work and the number of formal dinners attended, particularly by members of the cabinet. I'm convinced that research would prove that membership of the cabinet adds, on average, half a stone per year to the weight of a politician.

The good news is that although in Ireland we slag politicians off for putting on weight, we will still vote for them.

The Irish just don't like perfect people. We tolerate Pierce Brosnan because he can act, he comes from Navan and he seems to have his head together. But we look at a man like Liam Neeson with his busted nose and immediately figure he'd be fun to hang around with.

The guys who are popular in Irish TV culture tend to be the Brendan Gleesons of this world: the big, affable, rough-hewn style of person. We don't have much in the way of Hollywood heart-throbs and the ones we have, like Colin Farrell and Gabriel Byrne, we don't treat as such.

There are parts of the world where people will throw knickers at Bono and swoon at the very sight of him. In Ireland we see a lad with pink specs and say, 'Go away with yourself.'

There is sort of a rebel element to being Irish. The Irish media complained about Bertie's anoraks and trousers at half-mast until he got his wardrobe together. They felt it wasn't appropriate for the leader of the government to look like he'd been dragged through a hedge backwards. It never struck them that they're always moaning about politicians being inauthentic and when there was one who *was* demonstrably authentic, they wanted him to change. The general public was never that pushed about Bertie's clothes and in fact got quite a kick out of the canary-yellow trousers (with cream jacket) he wore at a G8 summit in Savannah, Georgia, in 2004: there's our guy refusing to wear the uniform and if those international leaders don't like it, to hell with them. That preference for the unusual, the individual, the maverick, the person who doesn't quite obey the rules, who won't kowtow to received wisdom, lies deep in the Irish genes. Most of the advice given to politicians about what they should wear is instinct dressed up as dogma and can safely be ignored.

12

A Bit of Craic

Coming up to general elections, political parties do private opinion polling. Or at least they *claim* to do private polling, when it suits them to make that claim. In at least one general election in the past, one political party announced with great enthusiasm that the findings (negative) of one of the major newspaper opinion polls just before election day had to be completely wrong, since the political party's own polling showed a different (positive) picture altogether.

What followed was an embarrassing outbreak of, 'You show me yours, since I've shown you mine,' and the political party became very maidenly about protecting its precious information. If it *had* precious and private information, which the newspapers at the time begged leave to doubt.

Internally, political parties use opinion polls conducted in constituencies in the run-up to an election to play divide-and-conquer among the candidates on the ticket in a particular constituency. Each candidate is told that the opinion poll revealed that voters in the area weren't terribly familiar with the candidate. That his or her name-recognition was down at floor level. That voters couldn't remember encountering them in the area at all, at all.

The moral lesson, usually hammered home by the national

director of elections, is, 'You're not working hard enough at local level. Get out there and wear out some shoe leather.'

The first or second time an individual has the dire results of a constituency poll shared with him or her and the moral lesson drummed into them, they are motivated to stir their stumps and work more committedly on the ground.

This kind of poll can, however, wear out its welcome as a motivational tool. One of the old stagers who decided to throw in the towel before the general election of 2007 took great pleasure, when presented with the 'results' of recent polling, in telling the director of elections where to stick them.

> You might fool some of the younger arrivals with that crap. You don't fool me. I've always worked like a dog on the ground, for all the good it's done me, landing me with the boredom and routine of a backbench position for more than a decade. Your so-called opinion polls always show me not doing anything on the ground. I learned long ago that these opinion polls are fiction and you know what you can do with them? Annoy poor eejit with your fictional research. And another thing. Don't think I'm stupid enough not to see what you're at and what you've always been at. You gave me shag-all support, money or otherwise, in any of my campaigns, even when I was in trouble with big spenders from other parties. You just relayed enough negative news from opinion polls to me to make sure I would blame myself if I didn't get through on election day. Well, go get yourself some other poor fart to torture.

While there's certainly a case for working hard on the ground and appearing in a professional way on local media, these opinion polls never seem to catch anybody doing anything right. They never confirm a candidate in any of their own strengths. It's always punishment dressed up as encouragement.

In fairness, it would be difficult to frame a questionnaire which would capture what Irish people really like in candidates. EU Commissioner Charlie McCreevy – a devastatingly good analyst of voting patterns – always maintained that Charlie Haughey's abiding popularity, despite being dogged by self-generated controversy, was due to the fact that the plain people of Irish love the smell of sulphur. They are drawn by people who are just a little bit iffy.

McCreevy's point applies to more than the late Mr Haughey. The voting public does likes the scent of danger and threat. The whiff of cordite. It's one of the reasons why Sinn Féin, in the direct aftermath of the IRA ceasefire, were so popular. But the smell of cordite diminishes over time and it remains to be seen if Sinn Féin as a socialist nationalist party without a connection to the 'armed struggle', will continue to be popular in the south.

One well-known government figure, prior to the 2007 election, complained to one of my colleagues that internal research had been quoted to him which indicated that voters did not see him as 'the kind of fella they'd like to go for a pint with'. Since this was a man who'd be happy to go for a pint with almost anybody, he found the verdict profoundly depressing. Again it shows that the Irish like imperfect people we don't think are likely to lecture us on policy and who might just be a bit of craic.

The 'bit of craic' litmus test is very interesting. It may have been developed in Ireland but has wider application. Bill Clinton is an impelling orator, a sexual athlete and a genius but, above all else, he is a person who always exuded the sense that – if you went for a pint with him – he would be a bit of craic. George W. Bush was elected, first time around, largely because the media regarded him as a bit of craic. Hillary Clinton, in sharp contrast, while she is clever, diligent and has a genius for political survival, never gives the impression that she would be a bit of craic.

While craic has wider application, it's particularly interesting and relevant in the Irish context. I think the word craic is a fascinating thing. The fact that a nation of people utilise a word to describe enjoyment spent in company says something about Ireland. No other nation has ever come up with such a word. Other countries talk about fun, about social life, about any number of variants on both – but we're the only ones who have a specific term to cover the concept of getting a bunch of people together and having a laugh.

There's that element about Bertie Ahern and also, people say, about Brian Cowen. There was even that perception in a grudging way about Haughey. You knew that if you were ever in a private situation with him, he'd be a bit of craic. He'd be scary but he'd be a bit of craic.

John Bruton was never a bit of craic. He was admirable. He was clever. He was full of ideas. But he was never going to be a bit of craic, whereas one of Enda Kenny's most attractive features is that he is undoubtedly a bit of craic. In fact, when it comes to Enda Kenny, he's nearly *always* a bit of craic, except when he's being serious and angry in Leinster House attacking the Taoiseach on some issue.

Which brings us to the limitations of political consultancy. If someone isn't craic, you can't inject that capacity into them. Some spin-doctors like to portray themselves as inventing the right personality for a candidate. It's a lie. You can't graft any personality trait on to a man or woman. They're hard-wired with their essential traits by adulthood. All you can do is to encourage them to display or not display facets of their character.

If a politician is a bit of fun, the more that you can allow that to be seen the better, particularly in Ireland where it is so important that someone is fun to be with. We value clubability and craic more than anywhere else in the world. In Ireland, in recent years, craic is one of the things that, in the absence of exciting issues differentiating the parties, has become increasingly important.

The 2007 election was an election of boredom, not an ideological debate. It was not about reinvigorating a nation brought to its knees or a rebellion against a rejected set of national values. It was not about fixing gross inequities in social welfare or even about getting the health system right, despite media emphasis on that issue, because: a) the Irish public is literate enough and well-informed enough to know that the collapse of public health systems is a reality throughout the developed world and; b) now the HSE has been set up, we have less expectation that ministerial intervention can make sweeping changes in individual hospitals.

We were bored by politics, now that the scandals had been played out *ad nauseam* in tribunals. The 2007 election was a choice between retaining the experience (of the incumbents) and taking a punt on an inexperienced administration – no matter how competent – at the ballot box. Experience won in the end – but only just.

13

The Myth of Body Language

Body language is not a complete myth. There are grains of truth in it.

A Chinese proverb that's been around a millennium or two, for example, suggests that a man whose stomach doesn't move when he laughs is not trustworthy. Good observation. Someone who's doing a pretend laugh, a social laugh, doesn't involve all the muscles required by what we – following the Chinese line of thought – have always called a belly-laugh.

Technically, body language is part of para-language, the range of ways we communicate outside of words. Anybody who has ever had a baby in their home knows that, long before they have words, babies communicate a wide range of feelings and needs. By crying. By not crying. By smiling. By swelling out their lower lip in a way that says, 'Something's not quite right here.'

Body language can be voluntary or involuntary. Gestures, smiles and other actions are often chosen by the communicator. Facial expressions and other indicators of how we're feeling or reacting may not be consciously created. They just happen.

Sometimes, in a tense situation, the way we use our bodies can send louder messages than the words we use. For example, in the lead-up to the 9/11 attacks on the Twin Towers, the men who were to pilot the planes that morning visited public libraries to send and receive e-mails and do research. In one of those libraries, in Florida, the librarian mentioned them to a colleague.

'What's their problem? I don't have a problem with them; why are they looking at me?' she wondered aloud.

She had registered that the men glanced at her more often than any normal library-visitor would have. In retrospect, it's pretty obvious that they needed to know a) that she was staying put at her station, b) that from her station she couldn't see what sites they were visiting or what messages they were receiving and sending and c) that she did not suspect them in any way.

None of them *said* anything. But their bodies said it for them: we're up to something here.

Body language has been studied, in the west, since the 1960s. This study informs psychology. It's known, for instance, that people suffering from profound depression tend to walk slowly, move in a hang-dog way, sit looking at the floor and smile rarely.

To coin a cliché, it's not rocket science. The problem is that it has been turned into a pseudo rocket science. Enough information has leaked into the public domain to convince television viewers that they can spot 'bad' body language and correctly interpret it.

A colleague of mine recently worked with a politician who then appeared on a current affairs TV programme. Several people later mentioned to my colleague that the politician was 'definitely uncomfortable and nervous'. The reason was that the politician's leg was in view and it jigged throughout the interview. I laughed when I was told about this. Because this man's left leg *always* jiggles. He could be discussing his baby daughter, the money he won at Cheltenham or how he hates his party leader. It doesn't matter. The left leg is in action. It's a tic. You know how sometimes your eyelid twitches for a couple of hours for no good reason? That's a tic. It has no emotional significance. It can be the product of tiredness, of the way you lay on the pillow last night, of mild neuralgia or of rubbing your eye too vigorously. But – like the man with the jiggling leg – if someone watching you on TV notices your eyelid doing its thing, don't be surprised if they attribute all sorts of obscure motivations to it.

Take the man with the jiggling left leg. The body language course will tell him this derives from tension (in fact, it's a habit), that it conveys the wrong message (which will confirm what he already knows and resents) and that he must eliminate it. Just how he's going to eliminate it will not be established. It's up to him.

Now, think about that guy's problem. Particularly if he's two months away from an election and is going to be on TV at least once a week during those two months. What's he going to do? Remind himself every three minutes to keep his leg still? The first problem with that is the negative feedback loop it creates. Every time he finds himself a-jiggle, while he's telling his leg for Chrissake to be still, another part of his mind is going to be criticising him and his leg for their performance on the programme up to then while wondering how many people have noticed and made negative judgements about his leg. All this is going to diminish or eliminate his capacity to concentrate on persuading voters that the policies he is trying to outline will change their lives for the better and that they should, accordingly, vote for him. He'd be much better to ask the TV stations to put him in a chair where his leg is not in full view of the camera or (worst case scenario) clip ankle weights on under his trousers to make it more difficult for the leg to get going.

The jiggling leg has no significance. It has, however, *attributed* significance, just as the position of someone on TV sitting with their arms folded will attract attributed significance. Viewers who have read anything about body language will snap their fingers (body language for 'Gotcha!' just in case you hadn't noticed) and attribute the folded arms to defensiveness, intransigence or terror.

Sometimes, people fold their arms because they are defensive, obstinate, closed or scared witless. But sometimes, they fold their arms because they've done all the other legitimate things they can do with their arms and this gives their muscles a bit of variety. Sometimes they fold their arms because they're cold. Gerry Spence, the American lawyer, once pursued a juror who had sat for two weeks in the jury box while Spence argued a case, arms folded the whole time. Spence – 'educated' by a body language course taken prior to the court case – asked the man if he'd been feeling negative about Spence's arguments throughout the case. The man shook his head and told Spence he thought the attorney had been making a lot of sense. Why, then, Spence asked, had the juror sat throughout the two weeks with his arms folded? The man looked at Spence as if he thought he must be daft. 'I got a big belly,' he told him truthfully. 'And a man's gotta put his arms someplace.'

That's not to say that certain physical behaviours cannot or should not be changed. Working with cashiers in a bank some years back, I noticed that when a customer came to the cash desk, the cashiers tended to say 'Be right with you' while continuing to do tots on their oversized calculators. That body language sent an unmistakable message to the customer: you don't matter to me as much as finishing the sums do. Once every cashier knew that the minute a customer hoved to, that customer was more important than the arithmetic and that the right thing to do was to abandon the calculator, the body language sent a message that matched an improved reality.

In order to cope with the uninformed interpretation of body language, more and more people, including politicians, who have to communicate in public, are taking body language courses. Unfortunately. There is wholesale peddling of body language tricks to politicians, each supposedly guaranteed to make them more likeable, more authoritative or (God between us and all harm) more statesmanlike.

This has been greatly, if inadvertently, helped by the media, because the media get so fascinated by stuff about 'physical tells'. A physical tell is a giveaway gesture, usually unplanned by the gesturer. Whole TV series have been created around spotting and interpreting physical tells and at least one pundit claims to be able to predict whether or not a couple will remain married or will divorce, based on the physical tells revealed in their wedding-day videos.

It's not rocket science either, the capacity to note and interpret physical tells. A client of mine, who works for a multinational, tells the story of her vice-president, based in Oregon, who makes regular, ostensibly purposeless phone calls to her. Except they're never really purposeless. The Veep talks casually about a number of issues and then slides in a question: 'How's John Brogan doin'?"

The first time it happened, my client hesitated, knowing that John Brogan (not his real name) had just been diagnosed with Parkinsons and was panic-stricken about the implications of the disease for his career and family life.

'That's fine,' the Veep said and rang off.

My client sat, flummoxed, trying to understand what had just happened. Eventually she realised that the vice-president was a genius at picking up small signals. Somewhere along the line, in a conversation with someone else at her plant, he had registered that something was slightly off about John Brogan. He had telephoned her to confirm it. Her hesitation was all he needed. He didn't have to force her to break a confidence: a pause of one-and-a-half seconds delivered the information he needed. That hesitation amounted to a 'physical tell'.

Physical tells can be – and sometimes should be – controlled. The unintended half-sigh an executive emits when a particularly verbose colleague arrives in front of their desk is a physical tell which can annoy the colleague. There may be better ways of communicating with her. It may, for example, be more productive to say, 'I'm in a complete stew over a report I have to have ready by lunchtime, so if you're not desperate to talk to me, could I ask you to take a rain check?' Some managers convince themselves that they are equally open and communicative with all their reporting staff, whereas they may be delivering what Professor Mary Rowe has dubbed 'micro-inequities': the split-second unintended gestures, facial expressions or sighs which don't amount to overt contempt but which can be picked up by the other person, consciously or unconsciously, and which influence the ongoing relationship.

Some people can gain hugely from body-language training. Those with hearing impairment, trained in sign, can not only communicate with others but join a mutually-supportive community of signers. People with Asperger's Syndrome have an impaired capacity to 'read' the physical signals the rest of us take for granted. They don't understand the facial expression that says, 'I'm bored rigid, you've been talking far too long, belt up, would you, please?' so they may continue a monologue, not because they don't care about the other person's needs but because they don't understand the physical expression of those needs. Parents of children who have Asperger's Syndrome or autism know that, through training, the child can learn that meeting someone's eyes is a good thing and that hugging their mother or father and telling them, 'I love you,' has a meaning their impairment would otherwise make them miss.

All that said, however, the fact is that much of body language as applied to politics is a myth without value or point.

There is a big risk that experts look at individuals with certain body-language features and isolate these features in order to impose them on other people. For instance, if you are Arnold Schwarzenegger in your prime, you have enormous latissimus dorsi (the wide muscles which run across the top of your back). Because you have them, you develop the body-builder walk, with the arms hanging wide. The body-builder has no choice but to let his arms swing wide, in order to avoid rubbing the skin of his oversized muscles raw.

However, not so long ago, some genius at over-interpretation of body language looked at this syndrome and took a quantum leap. 'That's how big strong people walk,' he said to himself. 'I know what I'll do. I'll make small weenie people walk the same way and that will convince everybody who sees them that they are really strong, that they are born leaders.'

One of the end results was that some leaders – George Bush, for instance – have developed a bizarre loping gait that they were not born with. Some idiot told them, 'This will make you look strong.' Instead, it makes them look at best odd and at worst half-witted.

These individual bits of illogical extrapolation without

any evidence lead to crazy dogma, sworn to by consultants on both sides of the Atlantic and purchased at enormous cost by political parties and individual politicians. Take the positions in which politicians stand for photos. The dogma is that the American President will always place you on his left when he's being pictured so that he can position his arm across his body while shaking your hand. This is supposed to send messages to the viewer's subconscious, alerting them to the power of the individual in the picture.

These things have so little to do with getting elected so it's bizarre that they get so much attention. But they become the things that most possess the mind of people. One Irish politician who shall be nameless was obviously told some time ago that, in a group picture, the person pointing the finger is the one everybody looks at. So in all photographs, there's Head-the-Ball, index finger stiffened. He's like a permanent personal signpost to the nearest Gents. In some pictures, because the rest of the participants in the photograph haven't been let in on his cunning plan, none of them are looking at him or at his finger, which isolates him and his finger as peculiarly as if he was knitting. Now and again, other people in the shot are captured looking at his extended finger as if it was a gun. Occasionally, because he was actually speaking at the same time as he was finger-pointing, the other people in the photograph are looking at him. The bottom line is that he's playing a silly trick to achieve an objective nobody has ever proven to be: a) possible; or b) productive even if it were possible.

Sweating is one of the physical tells of which observers believe they have the interpretation down pat. A politician who sweats is a politician who has been caught out. Or is just about to be caught out. Or who really *should* be caught out, because look at him, he's sweating, he must be guilty of something. (He could, of course, just be a natural sweater. Captain Bligh of the *Bounty* noted in his diary long before the mutiny led by Fletcher Christian, that Christian was a natural sweater. Bligh fastidiously observed that Christian sweated so profusely that he soiled everything he touched.)

None of this is to minimise the misery caused to its sufferers by excessive sweating. It can be a nightmare. A nightmare in the daytime, destroying clothes, creating odours, isolating the sufferer from others. Excessive sweating can be dealt with surgically. Other, less drastic corrective methods include injections of Botox near the sweat glands. The chemical, better known for its wrinkle-prevention capacity, paralyses the muscles which would otherwise be in overdrive and its use in sweat-minimisation is clinically proven.

A turbo-charged antiperspirant brand called Mitchum, available in the US in unscented cream form, can also be of topical use. A politician who knows they get dribbles of sweat at the temples or forehead in a tense situation or an overheated room (like a TV studio) can apply the cream to their face (prior to the application of make-up, in the case of a TV appearance) in order to prevent this happening. Mitchum, applied to the palms of the hands in advance of a job interview can be useful to applicants who dread the moment when their cold, sodden hand grasps that of the HR Manager or other recruiting executive.

Sweating can also be reduced by wearing natural fabrics like cotton and linen which breathe and wick perspiration away from the skin and avoiding fabrics which capture and increase body heat, like nylon and polyester.

While I'm on the subject of sweat, Tony Blair showed up at one famous gig where he was soaked in sweat. Perspiration pouring from his every pore. His clothes were visibly sodden – darkened in great obvious patches from sweat. Any image consultant would tell you it is a bad idea to be seen to be wringing with sweat at a political speech. Blair's popularity, according to this received wisdom, should have dropped like a stone. It didn't. The sweat-soak did him no harm and his popularity ratings went up, although, if Tony Blair made a habit of arriving at public events sodden with sweat, it might not contribute to his popularity over time.

The things that create the real difficulties for politicians are nonsensical interpretations of their body language, presented as if they were gospel truth, particularly in public analysis of the big TV debates between leaders of political parties close to an election.

For example, if one of the leaders puts his hand over his mouth, a commentator will state as fact that this establishes that the leader was lying at that point in the programme. It's common currency that touching your face, covering your mouth, playing with your hair, inserting your finger inside the neck of your shirt, fiddling with your signet ring, torturing a paper clip, shifting in your chair or wringing your hands are infallible proof that what you are saying is a lie.

It's common currency and it's complete nonsense. Take just one example: putting your finger inside the neck of your collar. The man who does this may do it for a myriad reasons. He may be just back from holiday and have sunburn the collar is hurting. He may have put on weight but bought a shirt in the size that used to fit him, so needs to ease its pressure on his jugular. It may be an habitual gesture he does when he's thinking.

There is no single physical tell which establishes that a man or woman is lying.

When I'm training detectives and HR professionals in how to detect lies, I emphasise that they have to start with a complete understanding of the individual's normal physical habits. If, for example, a man has the habit of touching his tie while he talks, the fact that he touches his tie in the DVD clip they're watching may have no significance at all, despite popular belief that it's a giveaway tell. Even if a man doesn't usually touch his tie but does so in the clip, that is not proof that he's lying. It may be an indication that he's tense. People get tense for all sorts of reasons, not just when they're telling fibs. And finally, the physical tell they observe must be linked to several other behaviours – some of them verbal – before you can have any certainty that the individual is telling porkies.

If a few simple tells were proof that someone it untruthful, we wouldn't need lie detection technology. But – and this is important – even lie-detection technology is not foolproof, which is why it cannot be introduced into a court of law. It may *indicate* dishonest behaviour but criminals who have learned to control their breathing and their reactions can defeat it.

It's easier, it's more fun and it sells more papers to do a piece on what a political candidate's body language supposedly reveals about them than to do a piece exploring what they stand for and why. Plus, it feeds into the concentration by media on 'character' which allows the commentator, in essence, to say to the reader or viewer, 'You see the obvious about this political figure but I'm going to tell you psychological secrets about him or her.'

The problem, from the politicians' point of view, is that they can have their reputation destroyed by the deployment of pseudo-science.

14

THE MYTH OF THE ARD-FHEIS/
PARTY CONFERENCE

The Ard-Fheis is important because it's one of the central pillars of the media's view of your party and of your party leaders. Ard-Fheiseanna and party conferences are no use for getting any individual candidate elected. They do, however, motivate the grassroots, which can be a horrifying thing to be near. The other benefit delivered by an Ard-Fheis is to put the party leader briefly on TV speechifying before the 9.00 news and if people are really bored or if the remote control is a long way away, they may actually leave him or her on.

An Ard-Fheis itself, for those who have never been at one, is stunning because people come out of the woodwork and out of bogs and mountains and forests and islands and climb out from towns that long ago fell beneath the sea to travel to the RDS or Leisureland or the Point. They wear their best brown suits and they arrive *en masse* four days in advance and begin getting royally pissed and they stay royally pissed for three-and-a-half days. They meet Micky Joe Finn who was the tallyman back when W. T. Kelly got elected in 1946 and remember how that was a great election. If they're drunk enough they get into the main room where speeches and discussions are happening and sleep aggressively at the candidates. I've never known the purpose of those discussions because nothing is decided and nothing is any different the day after but it all adds up to something very satisfying for those who attend.

The high point of the events is the state of frenzy which develops about six minutes before they release the leader into the hall, which at that point contains everyone attending the Ard-Fheis, or at least very single person who is still conscious and not *in flagrante* at that moment. They are all salivating at the prospect – not of the speech but of their chance to go absolutely mental at the first opportunity within the speech. Standard practice was that the candidate was preceded by the greatest headbanger the party can find. This is changing slightly now and sometimes the candidate is preceded by the prettiest female candidate the party can find or the one who best fits the majority demographic. Their job is to whip the crowd into a frenzy by saying all the things that can't be put on air. At the point when the audience is becoming incontinent with excitement, RTÉ announces that they're ready and the leader is released amongst them. At this point all hell breaks loose, loud music plays, the leader walks the gauntlet through flailing hands and begins the speech.

At this point no one in the hall is listening any more.

The people from RTÉ are fighting with people from the party about how long this is all going to take and everyone in the hall is waiting for their cue to roar. Actually it's like watching people watching an opera – they don't understand the language but they know that there is a certain high point at which they shout and they all sit braced waiting for something that will give them the opportunity to shout.

What it is that gives them the opportunity to shout depends on the skill of the speechwriter. If the speechwriter is good, they will shout at something that vaguely resembles policy. If the speechwriter is bad they will have to resort to erupting at any contemptuous message about the opposition. At which point they will go apoplectic again and with luck the guy at home who has lost the remote control will think the candidate is saying something important as opposed to uttering a tired whinge.

Twenty-eight minutes later the speech ends with a climax of screaming. Now, the objectives change. RTÉ's objective is to get everything packed up and get the hell out as soon possible and the party member's objective becomes: 'I'm up for election in the next six months in north Leitrim. I will doubtless seal the deal if I can be seen on telly or in the papers next to the party leader.'

So the biggest crush in the world commences. It looks like the Hillsborough disaster as they all jump up on the stage and manhandle the party leader for the next twenty minutes. The party leader just wants to go and get drunk – end of Ard-Fheis. At exactly that point, anyone who is useful to anyone leaves – RTÉ goes, the party leader's family goes. Anyone who is still conscious leaves and the descent into the ninth circle of hell becomes complete.

What's intriguing about the Ard-Fheis are the run-up to it and the various processes that fit around it, because this is such an embedded-in-the-camp event for the party that everyone has to be involved. The speech has to be written by at least nineteen people. Every one of those nineteen people believes that there are four critical issues. None of anyone's four issues overlap with anyone else's four but they are all equally important and they all must be listened to.

The party leader, if he is any good, has long ago learned that you don't say no to anyone because that will annoy people, so you end up with this log-jam of seventy-eight different items that must be included in the speech. The party leader isn't going to make the choice. Someone else's head has to be on the block as to which one gets dropped. This goes round and round the houses and more and more meetings are held to fight over the speech until it starts to crystallise into some kind of godawful form.

At which point the 'Oh, we forgot' syndrome begins.

We forgot to mention fisheries in Killybegs. Everyone in the room says in unison, 'To hell with fisheries in Killybegs.' Some guy whose job it is to monitor the health of the fishermen in Killybegs starts to give a briefing on how that's a swing constituency and how it's absolutely vital. Gradually fisheries in Killybegs, broadband, crèche facilities in north Leitrim – all these start to beat their way back into the speech.

At the same time, all the big decisions like what colour is the backdrop going to be and what will the issues that we debate be and who will be at the debates are farmed out to the nearest handy human, because a collective decision has been made without anybody noticing, which is: the only thing that matters in the Ard-Fheis is the leader's speech.

What *should* happen but what never *does* happen is that there should be one person in charge of collating all the stuff that comes in from everyone who wants to contribute a theme or who needs something covered by the speech. That person's job should be policy prioritisation or issue prioritisation. They should have the power to decide what's getting in and what's not getting into the speech and to explain to those who think they're going to die if their theme gets left out that there's not a big vote going to come in on that issue, so it has to be cut.

When the obvious inessentials have been cut, the standard speechwriter should have a go at it, ideally four weeks in advance of the Ard-Fheis. The first draft should be thrown at whatever consultant is relevant to see that it ticks the right boxes.

The key to a good Ard-Fheis speech is to have one theme. The thing that will make people say, 'Yeah, he fundamentally talked about X.' Often it's difficult for someone who is native, inside the political party, to move away from the specifics of lots of individual issues to say, 'Hang on, what's the overarching thing, what's the one thing that will set people alight?'

If you look at our great speeches of our time, wherever they were given, they talked about one fundamental idea that people rowed in behind. All too often an Ard-Fheis speech becomes a shopping list. You're all the time balancing boredom with issues, trying to find the way that will make people care about the specifics that you're raising.

Party HQ folk decide it doesn't matter if they audience are interested: they just have to be *told*. Tell them enough stuff they're not interested in and at the end of it they glaze over and the media glaze over too and become bored during the speech.

Overall what you're trying to do is to get media to make a subjective judgement about the leader: 'By Jesus he's good.' Once they've done that, they'll find the evidence to justify it. If you don't get them to make that, it doesn't matter how many of the boxes are ticked: they'll still write a negative piece about the speech.

A great speechwriter can be the catalyst for them to make this positive central decision. A great speechwriter knows their speaker. Knows their thinking, their background, their language, their references, their reading habits and their favourite music. A great speechwriter understands the differences between the written and the spoken word, so that what the politician gets is a speakable script, not a complex essay. A great speechwriter has a little of the theatrical director in them, a little of the musician, a little of the poet – and an amazing instinct for the emotions of the audience. But above all, a great speechwriter is anonymous, subordinating their personality to that of their speaker – and then shutting up about their involvement.

Great speeches move the audience, individually and severally. They make listeners see the world a little differently and want to quote what they've heard, so they ask for copies when the delivery is over. They change a politician's prospects, and they can change the thinking of a nation.

15

The Myth of the Lying Politician

Churchill frequently quoted Stalin's comment: 'In wartime, the truth is so precious, she should be surrounded by a bodyguard of lies.' Most politicians would deny it but the reality is that in politics the truth is so precious that it is frequently surrounded by a bodyguard of lies.

Voters constantly talk about the lies politicians tell but the reality is that politicians tell fewer lies, in any given day, than most people do. If you were to put a hidden camera in a room where a politician like Brian Cowen was having a meeting with a delegation, the first surprise would be how little the Taoiseach talked during that meeting. The members of the delegation would do the talking. Cowen would do the questioning. And the listening. And the nodding.

If you halted the delegation as they left and asked them about Brian Cowen's response, the overwhelming likelihood is that they would be enthusiastic. 'Oh, he completely agreed with what we proposed,' they'd tell you. 'He said he'd make sure it happened. He said –'

Now, you would know that Cowen had said the sum total of damn-all. He had, by his attitude and his attentive listening, given those present a sense of comforting interest, which they then transmuted into agreement with what they proposed. Half the people who complain about being misled by or lied to by politicians (not to mention spouses, partners and bosses) are people who didn't listen carefully enough to what was being said to them. Or not said to them.

Most people really lie quite a lot, even minor lying. Newspapers make much of the 'fact' that most of us utter as many as eighty social lies a day. Meaning that we say we're glad to see people when we'd prefer them to be in Singapore and admire a dress that makes its wearer look like a hand-stuffed draught-excluder. In fact, though, not even the 'social lies' we're all supposed to be guilty of every day are all deliberate untruths. Quite often, when we encounter someone we weren't looking forward to meeting, we realise they're not quite such a pain in the arse as we remember. Similarly, when we tell someone they're wearing a lovely dress, we may be factually accurate. It may be a lovely dress. It might even suit someone thirty pounds thinner and a foot taller. But the basic statement is true and its utterance in this situation motivated by a kind of kindness.

Because my company has developed courses to train detectives, barristers and HR interviewers in the detection of lies, we're often asked about how to spot a liar, as if it was a major scientific challenge. It's not, when people know each other reasonably well. Most wives, for example, will know when their husband is lying; most husbands will know when their wife is not telling the truth. They'll know this not because of some major specific body-language tic emerging when their mate is telling a porkie but because of a discomfiting *pattern* of behaviour.

With the exception of a few psychopaths who lie all the time without any particular gain to themselves, the general rule is that people lie only to get out of a tight spot or to get something to which they know they're not really entitled. Either way the risk of being found out looms, making the situation stressful and, in response to that stress, the liar acts differently. They don't always act in the same way when they're lying. Liars don't make it easy for the rest of us by making a habit of chewing nervously on a hank of hair or tapping their biro on their front teeth in a reliable 'Catch me if you can' physical 'tell'. But they do act differently from how they normally act.

This would suggest that it might have been easier to be a political liar in the past, when politicians had to deal only with the medium of print, as opposed to the current situation, when they must deal with a multiplicity of media. The fact that there is so much televised and broadcast coverage of politicians, particularly senior politicians,, means that people can notice when their behaviour changes. Although they don't always exercise the capacity.

It was notable, for example during the Mahon (Planning) Tribunal public sittings, that the overwhelming majority of the people who pitched up in Dublin Castle to watch the interrogations believed that all the politicians involved were guilty of corruption and lied all the time. Similarly with non-voters around election time: 'They're all liars, they're all the same, I wouldn't vote for any of them,' is the plaint.

It's an idiotic plaint. If you believe all politicians lie all the time, you're living in cloud-cuckoo land. Just because you're cynical doesn't mean you're wise. You can be just as self-deceiving as someone who is naïvely optimistic and positive about politicians. And you can miss the truth just as easily.

I have spent ten years of my life dealing with politicians of all parties, preparing them for radio or TV appearances or for the delivery of ard-fheis or party-conference speeches. During that time, I was never asked to help a politician to tell a lie and when my studio simulation uncovered one, the politician involved invariably abandoned it and was ashamed to have tried it on.

Aside from the self-protective, 'They're all lying all the time,' stance taken by some of the general public, the rest of us are pretty good at spotting political untruths when we see or hear them being uttered. (By the way, it's important to distinguish between a politician telling a lie he or she knows to be a lie in real time and an unfulfilled promise in a political manifesto. Now and again, a political party includes in a manifesto a promise it has no intention of fulfilling but for the most part, failure to deliver on promises made is due to unforeseen circumstances.)

When Bill Clinton claimed, 'I did not have sexual relations with that woman, Miss Lewinsky,' his wife may have chosen to believe him but most of the rest of us called it as a lie. We knew because the man who poked his index finger at the camera while he uttered the denial was not the Bill Clinton we were used to. Something is rotten in the state of Denmark, we assumed.

I said earlier that politicians probably lie less frequently than does the rest of the population. The main reason is pretty obvious: they're more likely to get caught. They live in a media-saturated world. A note-taking world. A world where a tape-recorder is always running, even if it's not being held out in front of them.

Take the instance of Minister Willie O'Dea and the taxi-men. The government had taken a stance on taxi-deregulation, which was as popular with taxi-drivers as ebola virus. Willie O'Dea, in his own constituency, met a bunch of taxi-drivers and shaded the truth somewhat in his conversation with them. The conversation was recorded. All was revealed. Willie got dumped on for not being honest but what was actually revealed was misjudgement. He should have figured that he wouldn't get away with it.

Many (not all of course) politicians who tell the truth in difficult situations cannot be credited with virtue but with good judgement and contextual awareness. They know they'll be caught. Sooner or later. Delayed exposure is almost like an electrical capacitor effect: the longer it lasts before it discharges, the bigger the bang when it does. For decades, loyalists within the Fianna Fáil party believed – many of them genuinely – that those who suggested that the late Charlie Haughey could not have legitimately earned the millions to support his lifestyle were making up bad scenarios, motivated by envy and political enmity. During that time, Mr Haughey got away with it. When, through a confluence of odd circumstances, he was revealed to have been on the take for years, it evoked an 'Oh my God' reaction from the party faithful. The world came crashing down around their ears.

On the other hand, the ones who are found out at an earlier stage experience a lesser bang because the false image didn't have so much time to build up. The lie did not store up as much of a charge before it exploded.

Politicians cannot always tell the truth. Finance ministers, for example, were always expected to deny that they had plans to devalue the national currency (back in the days when each country *had* a national currency) because to do so would have been tantamount to sacrificing the economy and the common good.

For the most part, politicians know that you can't be caught lying if you don't say anything. The problem, these days, is that media won't allow you to say nothing, especially if you have been a busy little media person up to that point, so politicians end up engaging in political waffle.

They often get away with it, too, largely because of a journalistic convention that has gone on long enough. In the past, when a politician waffled, a journalist – particularly a broadcast journalist – would pin the politician to the ground. The convention now is that it is enough for the journalist to show the audience that the politician is waffling so that the audience can draw its own conclusions without the journalist actually forcing the politician into a choke-hold. I think that's now outdated and we need to go back to the choke-hold.

In the summer of 2007 I listened to a radio interview during the controversy over Aer Lingus abandoning Shannon Airport as its base for flights to Heathrow. A west of Ireland Fianna Fáil backbencher came on the line, talking about his impassioned opposition to the abandonment – as he saw it – by the former state airline of a pressured region of the country.

'When this is pushed to a vote in the Dáil by the opposition, will you vote against the government whip?' asked the interviewer.

In response, you could hear the pitter-patter of tiny gurgles. 'Well, I don't want to pre-empt opposition thinking,' the backbencher said, incoherently.

'But will you vote against your own government?' the interviewer persisted.

The response was another set of pious generalities. The interviewer, at this point, clearly made the decision that his listeners knew the man was waffling because he didn't want either to lie or to fence himself into a corner. But this is to assume that the listeners will do the interviewer's job for him and allows the kind of waffle that results in a helpless cynicism on the part of listeners. Political liars should always be forced to answer the damn question and bolted to the floor if they lie. Sometimes this doesn't happen because the item is so overpopulated that the interviewer has to move on to the three speakers from other parties, rather than devote the necessary time to nailing the liar. Sometimes it doesn't happen because the interviewer doesn't listen closely enough. Sometimes it doesn't happen because the interviewer is happy that the item is *exciting* and doesn't care whether it reaches a truthful conclusion.

Whatever the reason for being able to get away with it, the first option available to an untruthful politician is waffle. Option two is to tell a lie with such extraordinary volume and panache that people begin to think the politician couldn't be lying if he's doing it with such conviction. It's an updated version of the observation by Hitler's propagandist Joseph Goebbels that a big lie that will always work rather than a small one.

The impact of the big lie, forcefully conveyed by a driving, dominant personality, is not unrelated to a form of trance-induction called 'shock hypnosis' where, instead of the usual approach to inducing an hypnotic trance, in which the hypnotist lulls someone into a passive and calm state, they effectively short-circuit someone's conscious thinking.

It works like this. You walk up to a total stranger in the street, stop your hand about three inches in front of their face and say, 'Your father says the wall isn't fully built.' They become so transfixed with confusion trying to figure out who you are and why you're talking to them in that way and how do you know their father that they get into a thought loop that pulls them out of reality – at which point they become very suggestible. If, at that suggestible point, you tell them, 'Now, you are going to walk into that shop and ask for a hat,' it's the only thing that seems to make any sense that they can latch on to and they just do it.

It doesn't work with everyone but there's a guy in England called Derren Brown who has made a big success out of a TV show where he does that kind of shock hypnosis, exploiting people's suggestibility. What George W. Bush seems to have done is to induce national shock hypnosis in the United States, an approach he developed with his former Deputy Chief of Staff, Karl Rove.

So the President goes out to Iraq an aircraft carrier, arrives in a US Navy S-3B Viking, wearing a flyer's jacket, unrolls a big flag that says 'Mission Accomplished', makes a speech to the stunned soldiers present and takes off back to the White House, while the entire nation does the equivalent of wandering into a shop to buy a hat.

None of it makes any sense. He isn't a flier. He never saw combat. The guys on that particular aircraft carrier have nothing major to do with the invasion of Iraq. The mission was to defeat terrorism but it hasn't had a dent made in it, while Osama is still sipping tea in an embroidered tent somewhere and dying his beard in order to look younger. Even if the mission *was* to pacify Iraq and introduce democracy to a nation that neither knew it nor wanted it, that mission hadn't been accomplished. Not when the invasion happened, in 2003. Not now. Yet, at the time, large chunks of the American populace bought the big lie. Shock hypnosis worked.

It had worked earlier in Dubya's career, too. Come out with an education policy when you're Governor of Texas called 'No Child Left Behind' that actually *causes* more children to be left behind than ever before in Texas history but call it loudly and repeatedly and enough people begin to believe it. That's what the current president did. It helped, of course, that he believed it himself – just as Ronald Reagan believed some of what *he* said that, objectively, was complete fiction, like his moving story of having been involved in D-Day in Europe, when in reality he was sitting in a film studio in Hollywood that he never left during the Second World War.

My research on lying introduced me to a man named Stan Walters, who is used by police forces all over America. Stan, who brands himself simply as 'the Lie Guy' told me, on first meeting, that the liars who are toughest to catch are the people who are psychologically unbalanced, because what normally allows a liar to be identified is their own stress at knowing they are lying. If someone has a pathology that means that they don't know or care that they are lying they have no stress and they're almost impossible to catch. A good example, in crime terms, was American serial killer Ted Bundy, whose grasp on the truth was minimal and whose self-confection was total.

You get the sense with certain political administrations that the truth has little merit and that lying carries so little fear or shame for them that there's no stress in doing it. Individuals, including the leader, can tell the big lie again and again and again with great volume and – here's the tragedy of it – eventually people begin to believe it. One of the most authoritative American commentators on the Third Reich, for example, said afterwards that he almost had to shake himself like a wet dog in order to free himself of the weight of lies he heard being told repeatedly when he was stationed within Germany during the early years of the war. Even though he was against everything the Nazis stood for, he found that the constant repetition of untruths influenced him.

In Ireland, we have a number of in-built defences against the big lie, although they are not unbreachable defences. Irish people have fallen victim to frauds of various kinds, notably financial frauds.. We buy stories – like the story of the woman who claimed to have been in a Magdalen laundry and whose book sold 300,000 copies before her family went public and said she'd never been near such an institution. We are, nonetheless, equipped – or at least we used to be equipped with an individual and group cynicism that kept us afloat like oil in the feathers of a seagull. We're always looking behind the statement for the real story. As my beloved godfather, Bunny Carr, once said to an audience of students in Harvard who asked him to define the difference between an American audience and an Irish audience: 'An American audience listens to what you say and an Irish audience wonders what you're getting at.'

Our national tendency is to parse any incoming statement, particularly from a figure who claims to have authority. 'Sez who?' we ask. 'Ah, bite me. I knew your mother. You're so full of it, you're standing in the overflow.'

Our final protection against the big lie is an well-developed sense of irony, the lack of which causes America such problems. They take literally what is said to them. We in Ireland, on the other hand, always assume a hidden agenda. Even if we believe in the general thrust of a politician's rally-the-troops speech, we cover up any enthusiasm we have, lest we be seen as uncool, unsophisticated and naïve. The desire to avoid appearing gullible is a huge factor in how the Irish approach any new issue.

Which in turn prevents literal truth-telling by some politicians. Take the issue of global warming or climate change, for example. The most authoritative scientists in the world have collectively said, 'This is it, lads. It's happening. No way around it. We can't stop it. But if we're going to slow it down so that life as we know it is still happening on this planet fifty years from now, we have to take radical action. Radical action is the only thing which will minimise the floods and catastrophes which will otherwise put millions of displaced refugees on the road, disrupting human life right around the globe.'

Now, when this major report comes out, who is Minister for the Environment in Ireland? The leader of the Green Party, John Gormley. A passionately-convinced environmentalist, no doubt about it.

If Ireland were to take a position of world leadership on this issue, which would be morally proper and – from John Gormley's point of view – absolutely the right thing to do, the Irish government would embark on a campaign to reduce air travel, starting by imposing the taxes on aviation fuel which traditionally have never been levied and moving on to an advertising and PR campaign designed to halve the number of business and pleasure air trips taken by Irish people in any given year.

The chances that John Gormley will do any of this are somewhere between slim and none. Because if the west of Ireland gets its knickers knotted about the removal of one route from Aer Lingus's portfolio of routes to Britain, claiming that its absence will cripple the economy west of the Shannon, how would the nation react to higher prices on Ryanair's cheapo tickets and a stated national policy of limiting travel on the part of the free citizen? Think somewhere between fury and mutiny.

John Gormley cannot even state that this is the right way to go, because if he were to make that statement, a number of things would happen:

- His own grassroots supporters would say, 'Well, why did we put you in there, if you know the right thing to do and you won't do it?'
- His Fianna Fáil and Progressive Democrat colleagues at the cabinet table would say, 'You're on your own,

        Sunshine.' Which would mean his resignation.

- Two days after his resignation, the media would write profiles of him positioning him as gullible and lacking in judgement to have taken the job on in the first place. Or – alternatively – for espousing so impractical a move.

Bottom line? The truth is rarely pure and never simple. To achieve anything, politicians must surround it with a bodyguard of nuance. But they still probably tell the truth a little oftener than the rest of us.

16

The Shadow of the Previous Guy

The overlap between media and politics is more than just the interaction between journalists and politicians. If someone becomes very successful, for instance, as a TV presenter or radio personality, the industry around them will misdiagnose why they are successful and try to replicate the person rather than the competence. This also happens in politics.

When you get someone like Jonathan Ross on BBC TV, suddenly every TV presenter tries to mimic Ross and what he does on his show. The same was true of Terry Wogan and Johnny Carson. Other broadcasters don't stop and say to themselves, 'Hang on. He's doing a series of things through his own personality. I can do those things in quite a different way. I don't have to do an impression of the guy.' This also happens in current affairs programmes where the interviewer's style of questioning is imitated.

The same is true of politics. The media talk a lot about 'honeymoon periods' in politics but it could be argued that when a new leader takes over, the opposite happens: a period in which the leader is compared, to their detriment, with the previous man or woman. Any strong personality at the top of a political party imprints their style on their followers and on the wider public, who subconsciously adopt that style as definitive or quintessential: that's what leadership is.

This is what happened when Tony Blair was in power in the UK. He was so successful that his great strengths, such as his capacity to sum up the moment in a phrase, or his competence on television, became the baseline for his successor. The feeling was that anybody who could not replicate the Blair style wouldn't be a 'real' leader.

It was even worse for John Major when he followed Margaret Thatcher. At any time, John Major, a clever and pleasant man, would have been seen as a tad understated in terms of presence and personality but following the Iron Lady, particularly because she had been in power for so long, he came across as grey, grey, *grey*. He hadn't a chance of walking out of the Thatcher shadow and of course she did her level best to ensure he could never succeed. Every time he seemed to be at a point of establishing an independent prime-ministerial life, she would intervene and pull the rug out from under him, reminding Britain of the didactic certainty she had always given them. Because Thatcher was such an iconic figure to the Tories, Major could not stand up and tell her to shove it. His responses to her interventions made his milk-and-watery image even worse.

Very strong personalities at the top of any political party tend to be followed by men or women who are markedly less strong and tend to have shorter reigns. Few people can name Franklin Delano Roosevelt's successor as US president, for example, because FDR had held the presidency of the US for an unprecedented (and unrepeatable) three terms, throughout major environmental and economic disasters like the Dustbowl and the Depression. He had brought America into the Second World War and out the other side as one of the victors. The photograph of FDR with Stalin and Churchill, taken at the

Yalta Conference in February 1945, is one of the most famous political photographs of all time. Small wonder that his vice-president, Harry Truman had a hard act to follow when he stepped into Roosevelt's shoes in April 1945.

It was slightly different situation when John F. Kennedy took over from Eisenhower in 1961, because, although Eisenhower had been a successful and revered general during the Second World War, he had been virtually invisible as president. His health was poor and he liked to spend time golfing. So by the time Kennedy succeeded him as president, it was almost as if the new man was taking over from a ghost or an absentee landlord.

In Ireland, the pattern of a big personality in power for a long time followed by a leader who is judged against the defining characteristics of the previous man was best seen in the transition from Charles Haughey to Albert Reynolds. Reynolds was a courageous man who dropped Ray Burke from his cabinet and who moved the Northern peace process decisively forward. However, Fianna Fáil had been trained into subservience by Charles Haughey. They were uneasy with a collegial, straight-to-the-point businessman after the grandeur and artistic sensibilities of the previous leader. Of course, it emerged later that the grandeur was based on gifts of money in brown paper bags and that Haughey had operated at a level of corruption unimaginable to the early Fianna Fáil leaders. Nonetheless, his style threw a long shadow. Many media figures, while acknowledging that he was a crook, felt that he was a colourful and exciting crook. Many of his own party found the aftermath of his rule dull and boring, as the conspiracy and intrigue dropped back to levels that are normal in any political party.

This reverse of the honeymoon period is an unnoticed pattern in most sectors, not just in politics. The man or woman who follows an iconic CEO faces months, if not years, of comparison with the previous incumbent. Board members, shareholders and staff watch the new CEO to see if they'll act like the old one did – and if they do, criticise them for lack of originality. It's a Catch-22 situation: everyone wants fresh thinking and a driving confident leadership but they don't want the positives of the previous administration abandoned, nor do they want it criticised in any way. Doing the job is not enough, as Carly Fiorina found out when she took over at the top of Hewlett-Packard, failing to read her board's signals. While she developed a stunning public profile for herself as a driving CEO readying HP to take over Compaq, she irritated the board and shareholders by her lack of reverence for the founders of the company and for the much-loved 'HP Way'.

The really difficulty of leadership style for a politician, however, arises when the leader is being compared to themselves. In an American presidential election, media will always fall in love with a politician who shoots from the hip without realising that this effect will essentially make them unelectable. Ross Perot and Ralph Nader are prime examples. People like the public person who shoots from the hip as long as they happen to agree with were the shot goes. The more you shoot from the hip the more chance that you are going to mow down a spectator and once you've done that you are going to get resented awful quick. Good politicians are the ones who pick the battles they are going to have. They choose where they can afford to be unpopular.

Mícheál Martin knew that the smoking ban was going to be phenomenally unpopular with the Fianna Fáil grassroots but he still went for it. Noel Dempsey's levy on plastic bags didn't require so much courage but is likely to be associated with him in the public mind much longer than some of the other policies he has pushed. Máire Geoghegan-Quinn, who was in politics for decades and in more than one government department, now surfaces in radio and TV programmes mainly because she hauled Fianna Fáil into decriminalising homosexuality in 1993, when she was Minister for Justice. In each case, the man or woman decided, for whatever reason: 'This is the fight worth having.' The bad politician is the one who shoots from the hip all the time and never gets to the position where they can have those fights that are worth having.

Ultimately, though, the dead giveaway of a bad politician is when they hate elections. There's a kind of politician who regards elections as an interruption in the proper order of what they should be doing, a pesky intrusion into a neat routine. Those politicians are in the wrong job. They should be top-level civil servants.

They're like the broadcasters who become famous doing some kitschy popular show, who immediately sneer at it and indicate they want to make documentaries. Here's the reality. *The Rose of Tralee* TV show embarrasses broadcasters, critics and columnists, who see it as a cringe-making leftover from a past that we are not even sure we had. But 750,000 people watch it. It gets one of the year's highest ratings in this country. Likewise, people give out non-stop about the *Late Late Show* and it gets the highest ratings of any programme of the country.

If the critics had their way, some of the most successful TV programmes would never have been broadcast (which might well have improved social life but the people, damn them, have their rights). If bad politicians had their way, they would never have to subject themselves to an election or tolerate public criticism. Great politicians, by contrast, *love* elections and are brought to life, even when comatose from exhaustion, by criticism. They want to go find the critic and pulp him. They want to announce that the critic is a Stickie from way back. They want their PR people to kill the radio producer who let the critic on the airwaves. But under all the bluster they love it, because they agree with Oscar Wilde's observation that the only thing worse than being talked about is not to be not talked about.

If you were born for politics, you will obsessively read and re-read every criticism made about you, knowing that every attack helps you and that when media ignore you, they murder you. Politicians die without light.

Many people who were decidedly *not* born for politics sucker themselves into it on a misapprehension. They see the coverage and buy into the notion of power and influence. More than anything else, however, they buy into the idea that politics allows you to be famous and liked. That's why some politicians choose their career. That's why some broadcasters choose their career. It never works, because any time you discover you are *not* liked – and it is likely to be often – is going to come as a thump in the face.

If you chose your career because you want power or an interesting high-paying job or whatever it might be then whether or not people like you is a side issue. Even politicians like Bill Clinton, Tony Blair and Bertie Ahern, who clearly got an enormous charge from 'working the rope' – physical contact with supporters and voters dying to shake their hands – were not in politics *just* to get that charge. It's a great benefit but it's not central. They need enough people liking them to be re-elected but they want to be re-elected *to do something* rather than just for the sake of being liked.

On the other hand, it appears that a groundswell of people who really, *really* dislike you can be a huge disadvantage. Professor

Drew Westen, whose book *The Political Brain* is fascinating about politicians' relationship with their voting public, says that once someone's attitude is crystallised into any kind of fixed position it is desperately difficult to change it. They'd much rather find a crazy rationale to support their pre-existing notion than change that notion.

So if you have a political candidate figuring in opinion polls as getting big chunks of 'Don't knows', that candidate is flying. Because 'Don't know' can be read as 'I might end up liking him', whereas if you get big chunks of 'Don't likes', that is really hard to reverse. The people who don't like a candidate will reconfirm their own beliefs to themselves, so whatever they hear they will interpret in a way that fits their pre-existing prejudices, along the lines of, 'Don't care what he's saying, he's a lying toad.' Successful political parties and candidates always have a solid core of people who would die rather than not vote for them, plus a large number of 'don't knows' who might be converted.

Whatever it is that makes voters give their number ones, twos or threes to one candidate rather than another, it's sure as shootin' not about qualifications. Which is ironic because the Irish government, in response to EU requirements, brought in a whole series of laws against discrimination and bias in hiring. They have tried to create meritocracy in the civil service with open and clear competency-based recruitment and promotion. Any experienced employer of any scale knows they'd better keep records of interviews conducted with aspiring employees so that they can prove, in the event of subsequent litigation, that the appointment was based solely on qualification and competence.

But the only people who don't have to answer any questions about qualifications and competences are the people who run the country because running the country is one of the very few jobs for which no one actually sets out to match someone's education and experience with the task they will have to do. So we have had Ministers for Finance who were solicitors and secondary schoolteachers. We have had Ministers for Health who were secondary schoolteachers and solicitors. For some reason, teaching and the law are jobs people want to get out of as soon as they qualify for them. Most of the escapees head for Leinster House. Many of them end up in ministries or as spokespeople in areas with which their education has at best a tangential relationship. The public effectively says, 'We like you and sure have at it.'

Politicians also get to break the rules about age discrimination. They say, 'I am young and I am new and I am fresh. I can connect with the young vote.' If you went for a job interview and said, 'Well, the key reason that you should give me this job is that I'm inexperienced and unknown and very definitely not an old fart like the wrinkly who currently holds the position,' the interviewing panel in front of you would throw an immediate wobbly. They would indicate to you that they could not talk to you any more about that issue and they would make careful notes so that they could later prove they had not permitted ageism to be expressed on their premises.

It's the same with family connections. If you went into a job interview and told the interviewing panel you had a great family and that your kids would help you do some of the work, the panel would look at you askance. They can't interview you on those private issues. They can't, when they look at your CV and notice you are a bachelor of forty-two years of age, fish around to see if you are gay. Nor can they ask you about your religion. Yet politicians are asked about the breakup of their marriage. Other politicians practically link arms with Sunday Mass-goers to establish that they, too, go to Mass. More than one single male politician has had to state, publicly, that they are not gay, when they were well within their rights to answer questions about their sexual orientation with: 'None of your business.'

Anyone going into politics should think long and hard about the degree to which they will sacrifice their private life. Too many politicians start out sharing everything and as time goes on, as relationships break up, as their children hit puberty with all its attendant excitements, try to reverse out of sharing.

Reversing out of sharing is impossible.

17

The Myth That Spin Wins Elections

Spin-doctors have moved centre-stage in the last few decades. Thanks to people like Karl Rove, James Carville and Alistair Campbell, there is now a sense that the people behind the scenes win elections by selling politicians like products. That is not how it is. That is not (with a few exceptions) how it ever was, and that is not how it should be.

Most CEOs and big companies have spin-doctors either on staff or hired externally. They advise on investor relations, they write speeches, they prepare executives to give interviews and they help to define the marketing and publicity plans of the company. They don't run the business, they don't make decisions about corporate direction and they don't hire and fire. They help the people who make those decisions communicate them. That's all.

The glorification of communications consultants is unnecessary for the consultant – we get paid whether people know what we do or not – and damaging for clients – it creates an impression that they are somehow unable to just 'say it straight'. The glorification also creates an overblown myth around the impact a spin-doctor can have. The story – probably apocryphal – is told of Jeff Skilling, CEO of Enron, saying, as collapse was imminent, 'This is a PR problem. Where is my PR department?'

As if spin could undo years of felonious behaviour.

The chairman of my company, Tom Savage, once described communications consultants (or spin-doctors) as being in the 'transport business': taking the best of a person and transporting it to a target audience, taking how a person communicates in a comfortable environment and transporting it into the pressured environment of a press conference or current-affairs studio. Good communications consultancy lies in the transport of a person's ideas and character, not the creation of ideas and the falsification of character.

The current public focus on spin, not policy; on campaign, not candidate, is a function of the twenty-four-hour news cycle. If you're a broadcast, print or web journalist, you have to file copy or put a show on air even if you have nothing to talk about. It is more than seventy years since a news broadcaster admitted that nothing had happened worth talking about. (It was Good Friday 1930 when a news announcer on the BBC introduced the broadcast by saying, 'Ladies and gentlemen, there is no news tonight, so here is some music.' He then filled the time with the delicate sound of piano tinkling.) Since then, the amount of news and the number of news analysts have increased exponentially and none of them will ever say, 'There is no news tonight.'

This ubiquity of media precludes a focus that is primarily on the candidate or the party's policies for the simple reason that you can exhaust the core of both within three days. Barack Obama's election as President of the United States is a good example of this. Once it became established that he was going to bring in a middle-class tax-cut, get out of Iraq and do his best to make health insurance available to all, that was the policy stuff all soaked up. Befor long we'd got all we could handle on his Kenyan home, Hawaiian granny and wife and kids. The only new elements in a campaign that went on for such a long time become the 'how' of the campaign, rather than the 'what'. How will Obama sell the tax-cut? How will he respond to Republican attacks? How will he show that universal health insurance isn't socialism?

To address those 'how?' questions, you need polls and commentators and the two sets of people who should be kept in darkened rooms and fed buckets of fish-heads end up centre-stage. When, *post factum*, the election is analysed, victory or defeat are attributed to the 'how' not the 'what'.

This devalues the politician. Obama is the perfect case in point. His campaign communications were handled superbly. He chose his target voter well (aiming squarely for the pressured middle-classes). He kept two consistent themes throughout the campaign (change and hope). He handled negative Republican attacks perfectly (highlighting them rather than directly retaliating) and his speeches, interviews and debates were exemplars of how such political communications should be handled. The 'how' of the Obama campaign was nigh-on picture perfect. But it was not why he was elected. And it would be a shame for hindsight to make it seem so.

When Obama was trailing in the primaries, I had the pleasure of talking to his foreign policy adviser, a Harvard professor and Pulitzer-prizewinner originally from Dungarvan, County Waterford, named Samantha Power. She subsequently resigned from Obama's campaign after a Scottish newspaper published an off-the-record quote from her calling Hillary Clinton a 'monster'. I had a conversation with her while we waited for a sound engineer to come into an RTÉ studio so I could interview her for the following day's programme. For fifteen minutes this brilliant woman talked about Obama.

'Could you imagine?' she asked, 'a Harvard law graduate who speaks Swahili as President of the United States?' She talked about how he listened, how he would personally thank her for work she did for him. She talked about his insight, his intellectual brilliance, his decency. At that point, he was not sure even of winning the Democratic nomination, never mind the Presidency, but here was a highly-educated, thoughtful woman whom *Time* magazine described as one of the world's 'top 100 scientists and thinkers' talking about a presidential candidate as one of the best and most brilliant people she knew.

She talked about him that way because she knew him personally. From that point on I knew that Obama would win – if his spin-doctors could accept that they were simply in the transport business. If they could transport that personal connection with the man to the millions needed to elect him, he would win, not because he spent more, or wore better suits, or had better soundbites: he would win because a nation would see what Samantha Power saw.

That's what the task is. It's transporting an individual to the millions of individuals who will ultimately elect him or her. That transport job now means downloading a candidate's thinking and converting it into speeches, into features, into video scripts. It means planning a route through the jungle of interwoven media to the end voter. It means deciding how to rebut untruths and skirt prejudice. But all the time the goal has to be the creation of an individual connection between two people. Candidate and voter.

For many years doing that in Ireland has meant talking through a filter. Almost everything a political candidate says is fed through a gauze of journalists, editors, broadcasters and producers. It doesn't matter how brilliant the speech in the Dáil is if a producer doesn't play a clip of it. It doesn't matter how well-argued the policy document is if the journalist can't be convinced to report on it. It doesn't matter how passionate the vision is if the presenter won't discuss it.

It makes the transport job more difficult. But we are at a turning point in Irish political communications. Generation X in now in its thirties. It has babies, houses, mortgages and jobs. And that means it votes. It is the first generation that sees peace in the North as the norm, not a novelty. It is the first generation that does not wear its Civil-War allegiances on its sleeve. It is the first generation driven by aspiration, not survival. And it is the first generation familiar with a new form of mass communication.

Generation X listens to morning radio in the evening as podcasts on their iPods. Generation X saves its TV viewing on to a hard disc and watches it when it suits, not when it is broadcast, thereby excluding itself from the passive prison of four channels and home-grown current affairs. Generation X sees current affairs as interactive, not declarative, texting live programmes for answers to its questions. Generation X writes its own encyclopedia. Generation X comprises, in large part, selective researchers who assume that primary source material will be available to them when they want it.

If someone from that generation hears about the medical-card controversy that blew up after the budget of October 2008, they are more likely to fire up a PC and search Google News than they are to buy a newspaper. If someone from that generation hears about Jonathan Ross being suspended for something he said on Russell Brand's show, they won't wait until the news covers it. They'll visit YouTube and make up their own minds. That generation is the first to view current affairs media as a combination of entertainment and research guide. They want their current affairs to be interesting and to point them to primary source material on which they can then form an opinion.

For Irish politicians this provides the biggest opportunity and the biggest threat for generations. It is a threat because political parties tend to be slow to change. They lack the daily incentive available to a company in the form of a profit and loss account; they are measurable only at elections, not on weekly performance, which dulls the urge to experiment with new approaches. It is years since retailers installed CRM (customer relationship management) systems to track, analyse and segment customers. No political party in this country (to my knowledge) has done the same. Despite having the biggest market research machine in the nation, none of them hold centrally, segment and use voter data garnered on the doorsteps. New technology is therefore a threat. Faltering steps are being taken by Irish politicians – the odd Bebo page here or web-video there – but the kind of integrated old and new media campaign waged by Barack Obama has yet to make an appearance. And that's where the great opportunity lies. For the first time in centuries the transport job is being reversed. No longer does the challenge consist of transporting the candidate to the voter: now the challenge is to transport the voter to the candidate.

It is easiest to explain this by way of analogy. Thirty years ago it was as if you had a conference hall stuffed with voters. And one by one (via newspapers, radio, TV and canvassing), candidates and commentators would appear before the crowd and try to sway their opinions.

This has now been reversed. The room is packed with candidates and commentators, all clamouring for the attention of the single voter in the centre of the room. That voter gets to select who to listen to and who to ignore, because the candidates and commentators now all talk at the same time, constantly.

The spin-doctor must now find ways to persuade the voter to listen to their client, then make sure their client can effectively say what they mean in a way that will keep that voter listening.

We're moving to a place where people can engage directly and virtually with politicians, where video can be made accessible without the filter of a broadcaster, where audio doesn't need a radio station and where opinion pieces don't need a journalist.

The key to the next election will not be recognising (ten years too late) that local radio is important, it will be recognising that the next generation is a swarm, whose thinking and decisions are influenced by a constantly shifting, constantly overlapping, constantly buzzing hive of information – all of which is interdependent, all of which is selected or rejected by the receiver and all of which feeds back into itself in a constant loop.

It is the biggest shift in Irish political communications since de Valera said of the new medium of television: 'Like atomic energy, it can be used for incalculable good but it can also do irreparable harm.'

This shift will mean that politicians face a communications challenge never seen before in this country or any other. And it is a shift that will make the transport business more interesting than ever.